How to Start Your Online Business Without Any Investment, Qualification and Experience

By

Amir Anzur
Talha Naveed
Mohsin Naveed

COPYRIGHT

DEDICATION

This book is dedicated to you, the reader who is ready to capitalize on the Internet economy.

If it weren't for you, we wouldn't have taken the time to write this book.

Thank you for picking it up, and please pass it on to friends who might also want to create wealth and benefit from this book.

ACKNOWLEDGMENTS

A special thank you to all the "angels" involved in helping us to develop our careers and this book - our parents, brothers, sisters, cousins, investors, colleagues, employees, suppliers, clients, followers, fans, teachers, mentors and friends. There are far too many people to thank and at the risk of leaving people out, we hope you know who you are and we thank you as always for your support.

BOUGHT ONE. GIFTED ONE.

We believe education is a right that everyone should have. If you purchased this book, we thank you. We have printed and distributed another copy to an emerging part of the world, as a gift on your behalf.

We hope the person who receives it will appreciate your gift as much as we hope you appreciate this book.

ABOUT THE AUTHORS

 **Talha Naveed** is a freelance writer and editor. He is one of the key contributors at PLDx.org - an online social platform that connects alumni of Harvard Business School from all over the world. He completed GCE A level from Roots Millennium Campus and he is currently pursuing a bachelors degree in Chemical Engineering from the National University of Science and Technology (NUST) - class of 2020.

Contact:
www.linkedin.com/in/talhanaveedtn
www.facebook.com/talha.naveed.957
email: talhanaveed.tn@gmail.com

 **Mohsin Naveed** is a freelance interpreter and writer. He completed high school from Roots Millennium School, Foundation in Engineering from NCUK, UK and is currently pursuing a bachelors degree in Petroleum Engineering at the University of Portsmouth, UK.

www.linkedin.com/in/mohsin-naveed-15a64070
www.facebook.com/mohsin.naveed.161
email: mohsin.naveed@valpo.edu

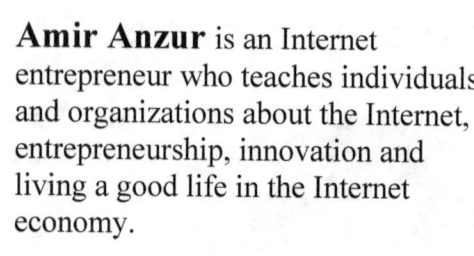

Amir Anzur is an Internet entrepreneur who teaches individuals and organizations about the Internet, entrepreneurship, innovation and living a good life in the Internet economy.

He won the 2005 European Prize for Innovation and his clients include Amazon, Google, Intel, Oracle, Xbox and Samsung. He is Co-Founder of mindGigs.

Amir has an MBA with Distinction in Leadership from IMD Business School in Lausanne, Switzerland; a first-class honors in Computer Science with Business and Management from the University of Manchester, U.K.; and an International Baccalaureate from the International School of Brussels, Belgium.

You can learn more or subscribe to his blog at www.AmirAnzur.com.

www.facebook.com/amiranzur
www.twitter.com/amiranzur
www.LinkedIn.com/in/amiranzur
www.youtube.com/amiranzur

CONTENTS

1. LESSONS FROM GETTING A HAIRCUT

If you go for a haircut in Lahore, Pakistan it will cost you 100 rupees ($1. Please note: all dollar figures are U.S.). A similar barber in Dubai will cost you 25 dirhams ($7). Get the same haircut in Geneva, Switzerland and it will set you back 40 Swiss francs ($45).

Is Jean-Pierre, the Swiss barber, really 45 times better than Imran, the Pakistani barber? Would Jean-Pierre make your hair look 45 times better than Imran?

We have had haircuts in different parts of the world and can say the results haven't been much different. Swiss barbers don't make you look 45 times better than Pakistani barbers or six times better than Emirati barbers. The experiences are different, but even that depends more on the individual barbershop than on the city. A high-end barbershop in Pakistan offers a similar experience to a high-end barbershop in Switzerland – but at a fraction of the price.

The Swiss barbers are making 45 times more than the Pakistani barbers for the same work and the same time. If anything, the Pakistani barbers have more time for a chat and might even give you a free head massage. Even if we adjust for higher rent, wages and other expenses in Switzerland, the Swiss barbers are making at least 10 times more than the Pakistani barbers while providing the same service.

Now you may ask: "What does a haircut have to do with creating wealth from the Internet?" As you read on, you will discover many of the lessons from the barbershop carry over to the digital age.

Jean-Pierre was protected in the old economy. Imran the barber could not compete for Jean-Pierre's customers. Imran didn't have a Swiss work visa, or the capital to rent a shop in Switzerland. Not many Swiss are going to fly to Pakistan to get their hair cut – even if it is 45 times cheaper.

But let's say, instead of haircutting, the job was video editing. Or graphic design. Or software programming. Or customer support. Or math tutoring. Or a number of jobs that didn't exist a few decades ago but are now essential. This change in the economy largely took place just in the last 15 years; the world is only beginning to realize the impact for the next decade.

The (non-barber) Jean-Pierres will face trouble now that their jobs are not location-dependent, while the Imrans will have opportunities. Jean- Pierre can no longer charge his local customers 45 times what Imran charges, unless, of course, he has a trusted brand, strong relationships, a production process unique to his locale or significantly better service. But the Imrans of the world can now get in the game. The Internet means they are no longer restricted by their passport and can serve customers in Switzerland, or anywhere else across the globe, from their home villages. This means their home countries can avoid the brain drain that plagued them in recent history.

Questions of Inequality

One question that might have occurred to you is: "Why are some people rich and others poor?" The average American earns over $45,000 per year, for example, while an average Pakistani earns less than $1,000 per year.

Why does poverty happen? Why is one person a millionaire and another living without running water? Is it genetics? Is it culture? Why are Africans "poor" and suffer from famines? Why is China's economy now booming and what could other countries learn from it? Why is it that one out of every four dollars spent around the world is by an American (US population: 300 million) while the rest of the 6.7 billion share the other 75% of the wealth?

We know you may not expect such deep, difficult questions at the beginning of a book about the Internet, but it's important to understand these ideas before we discuss the modern economy. When you truly understand exactly what wealth is, you will see exactly how big the impact of the Internet is and will continue to be in many societies and industries.

The Internet, like the telephone, the automobile, electricity and TV, is a tool that can help us reach our goals faster. We need to first understand what we want to use these tools for before we can use them effectively.

Peter Drucker, a management guru of the last century, said: "There is nothing so useless as doing efficiently that which should not be done at all." So we need to ensure the Internet adds benefit to our lives before we try to use it.

Or as Friedrich Nietzsche said: "He who has a why can endure any how." The point of this book is to get you to truly understand the "why," because the "why" of the Internet will give you a chance to create substantial wealth wherever you live and whatever your education level or financial background. Not only that, but it can help end global poverty. Once you understand the "why," the "how" becomes much easier to figure out.

If you were to take up golf, the first thing you would do is learn the rules of the game. You would need to know, for instance, that you couldn't throw the ball; you have to use a golf club instead. You need to know that you have to get the ball into the first hole first, and the 18th hole at the end. Once you understand the rules of the game, you can start improving.

If creating wealth is the game you want to play, first you have to understand the game. What exactly is wealth? How can we make more money? Why are some people "poor" while others are "rich?" In summary, how can we create more wealth for ourselves and maybe even help our neighbors to create more wealth?

As entrepreneurs we have spent many years traveling to different parts of the world, where we have witnessed great wealth, but great poverty, too. So the question of inequality has bugged us for a while. And if you start thinking about a problem long enough, you start to come up with solutions.

We have spent tens of thousands of hours figuring out how to create wealth online. We have worked with successful global companies (such as Google, Oracle, Samsung, Microsoft and Intel), governments (such as those in Abu Dhabi, Dubai, Pakistan and United Kingdom) and international associations (such as the World Trade Organization) to understand the bigger picture of wealth creation. We have worked with many millionaires and billionaires, but also spent time with beggars on the streets of Delhi and homeless people in London.

Between the two of us we have started companies in the U.S., the U.K., the U.A.E., and Pakistan. We were educated in the U.S., the U.K., Canada, Belgium, Pakistan, Switzerland and the UAE. The book is meant to give a global perspective on wealth rather than one specific to any country.

We invested time learning how to create wealth, knowing that someday we would go out and teach others. This book is an important part of our teaching. The simple conclusions you read in a few hours took us thousands of hours to figure out. We have distilled the lessons we learned from hundreds of books and many fine teachers, only some of whom we were able to mention.

Whether you are Ethiopian or German, the Internet gives you a chance to create wealth for yourself. But this book isn't about "how to get rich quick." If you're looking for a quick score, buy a raffle ticket and hope for the best. This is more about slowly building riches. The principles discussed in this book will prepare you to win in the Internet economy in the next decade. This could mean finding a life partner, educating your children, creating a living or advancing a cause.

The only way to truly create wealth, though, is to take action. Knowledge, like money, doesn't mean anything in itself; you must use it for something.

The funny thing about humans is that they will do more for others than they will do for themselves. If you tell parents to quit smoking because they are harming themselves, the response might be lukewarm, but if you tell them they are harming their child, they are more likely to listen. Read this book and take action for others; the wealth you create and the lessons you pass on will only appreciate in value.

Is Wealth Possible through the Web?

The founders of Facebook are the youngest self-made billionaires in history. In under a decade, Facebook is valued at a similar level as General Motors and McDonald's, who have hundreds of thousands of employees and took decades to reach the same level of success.

The founders of Google, eBay and Amazon have all also became billionaires in the past decade.

A website you might not have heard of — Diapers.com — sells $500 million worth of diapers through the Web every year. Zappos.com sells over a $1 billion worth of shoes through the Internet every year. Millions of people are being hired through Upwork.com and Elance.com. These sites make it possible for businesses in the richer areas of the world (e.g., North America and Europe) to hire people directly from poorer parts (e.g., the Philippines, India, Kenya, Pakistan, etc.). No visa issues. No minimum wage. Minimal hiring and firing costs. No flight costs. Zero telecommunication costs.

Clickbank.com has paid out over $2 billion in sales commissions for digital information products, yet is probably another website you haven't heard of.
Singer Justin Bieber can thank YouTube for launching his career and becoming a 15-year-old millionaire.
Some internet entrepreneurs share openly online how they make money and teach others, such as Pat Flynn of SmartPassiveIncome.com who makes over $55,000 per month, Steve Chou of MyWifeQuitHerJob.com who made $100,000 in sales from an online store and Andrew Youardian of ecommercefuel who made $1.3 million from his online stores.

We are not based in Silicon Valley, and our words are not aimed at California insiders who invested millions of their own dollars and realized the Web's potential a good decade before the rest of the world. This book is for the rest of the world.

A detailed analysis of France's economy over the past few years found that the Internet destroyed 500,000 jobs. At the same time, though, 1.2 million Web-based jobs were created, which is 2.4 jobs for every one destroyed. The point is, you can see the Internet as a threat or an opportunity. We hope by the end of this book you will see the bright side of the digital economy, which, even if it doesn't benefit you directly, will give your children a better future.

So although a Jean-Pierre could see his job disappear as an Imran can do it much cheaper and/or better, it also allows a Jean-Pierre to now move on to a different job or find a different way to generate wealth for himself. The basic economics of supply and demand are not changing. The Internet can significantly increase supply and demand. The place you were born in or your passport is no longer going to determine the wealth you create for yourself as the Internet enables more people to compete.
A Jean-Pierre might have had a better education than Imran in the past, but this is no longer the case. Anyone with computer access can visit websites such as KhanAcademy.org, YouTube, Wikipedia, Google and WebpreneurAcademy.com.

Before the Industrial Revolution, the normal thing to do was to go into the family business. If your father was a shoemaker, chances are that you would become a shoemaker. With the advent of machine- based production, the more respected thing to do was to work in a large corporation or to be employed by the government.

Smaller, more creative companies will flourish in the next decade, as governments and large corporations begin to cut employees. Larger organizations may make the same revenue, but they won't need as many people. Small is becoming the new big.

Your parents did not make a living through the Web. Chances are they were not entrepreneurs, either. This might make it difficult for you to envision a life working from home making a living off a virtual world.
You are used to seeing people go to work five days a week. Wearing a suit. Going home at 6 p.m. Collecting a paycheck at the end of the month. If your parents stopped going to work, they stopped getting paid.
If you want to become a Webpreneur, you will need to understand how the new economy works. Your parents and teachers might not be the best source of knowledge about Internet careers. Go out into your community and meet a real-life Webpreneur. Go to seminars. Buy courses or books online. Experiment. Only then will you truly believe that starting a business is possible and convince yourself to take further action.
The world is full of skeptics, so chances are if you want to go for something a little unusual, people will laugh at you. Look around and see if those people are living the life you want in the future.

Maybe you are surrounded by people who work in office cubicles all day, every day. Or by people who haven't had much financial success. If you have bigger plans that can help change the world, you might have to break away from these people. The whole industry is so new you need to do your own discovery.

If you are out of school, you need to realize that in the knowledge economy you will be an eternal student. In order to make a living, you will need to continually invest in your learning. The end of studying is not the day you received your certificate.

Even if you are in school, the information in this book is not yet taught in your curriculum. It will open your mind to a set of careers your teachers probably didn't know existed. The Internet gives the learner more power. Rather than having a teacher dictate learning terms, you can choose what you want to study, where you want to study and when you want to study: heck, you can even choose your teacher.

And if you are a teacher, this book will help you cope with the constant change of this era while preparing the next generation to succeed.

2. HOW TO TRAVEL THROUGH TIME

In the movie *Back to the Future*, Marty McFly (Michael J. Fox) is able to travel to the past and the future in a time machine. The ability to travel through time brings many benefits. For instance, the character of Biff takes a current sports book into the past and bets on sports games. He creates a lot of wealth for himself, as he already knows which team will win.

You can also travel through time. For instance, visit Abu Dhabi and you can smoke indoors in many restaurants. Ask Emiratis what they think about the impending smoking ban in 2012 and they might say: "That will never happen. Arabs love to smoke too much."

The Irish said the same thing in 1999. They also thought a ban would never happen in Ireland. The Irish loved smoking as much as the Arabs do. Dublin instituted a smoking ban in 2004. London and Paris followed suit, and in 2010 smoking was banned in Dubai – just up the road from Abu Dhabi.
The smoking ban started in Beverly Hills, California in 1987. If you want to see Abu Dhabi's future, at least when it comes to smoking indoors, you can visit California. And if you are Californian and you want to see what the past was like, visit a restaurant in Abu Dhabi.

Knowing the future is beneficial for entrepreneurs. In the U.K., for instance, the smoking ban meant restaurants could no longer count on fresh cigarette smoke to mask stale carpets or other odors. Dublin- based businesspeople could take advantage of the looming demand for fragrances that would be required in London (and Paris, for that matter). They could, in essence, predict the future.

We can predict the impact of the fast-food industry on many Arab countries. In America, McDonald's, Burger King, Coca-Cola and similar fast-food brands have been popular for decades. As a result, America is one of the most obese countries in the world; over 30% of its population is overweight. As fast-food franchises spread to the rest of the world, we can take steps to ensure our populations do not develop these health problems. We can learn from the past about junk food.

We can also see how other innovations and ideas diffused throughout society. Electricity, the telephone, the printing press, TV, radio and airplanes all spread across the world at different speeds. These innovations impacted each society differently, moving jobs from one industry to another — and making money for those who were prepared for the change.
You might be living in a place where the Internet is not a big part of your life — yet. Just as electricity and mobile phones spread (and continue to spread) across the world, so will the Internet. Perhaps you live in a place where you still book airline tickets through a travel agent. In the U.S., most people book their own airline tickets online.
There are people who benefit from any innovation and others who lose out. You, too, will lose out unless you adapt.

The former presidents of Egypt (Hosni Mubarak) and Tunisia (Zine El Abidine Ben Ali) could have seen the impact of the Internet on politics. In February 2008, John McCain, the American presidential candidate, raised $11 million for his political campaign using traditional fundraising methods. In the same month, Barack Obama went to zero fund-raisers and raised $55 million primarily through the Internet. Obama took advantage of the Web not only to help him raise money, but also to successfully direct his campaign volunteers and followers and ultimately get elected.

Many Arab leaders underestimated the Web's power and were surprised when their people organized and overthrew them. The Internet will continue to have a huge impact on governments, as it gives people a way to connect and organize like never before.

You can take advantage of the Internet no matter where you are, unlike the smoking ban, in which you suffered if it hadn't come to your part of the world yet. If you are based in a developing country such as Sudan and don't have many Internet users in your community, you can still market to foreign consumers. You do not have to emigrate to a major city to derive your income from there.

Ideas don't spread around the globe instantly, and Webpreneurs are taking advantage of this lag, which is called arbitrage. The website Groupon.com, for example, offers its subscribers high discounts in order to get volume sales for its business partners. A $100 treatment at a beauty salon, for example, might sell for $50 on Groupon. The salon would get $25 from the sale, and Groupon would get the other $25. The consumer would save $50. Even though the salon gets only a quarter of the original price, it benefits by attracting more traffic. It can then turn visitors into repeat customers. Groupon is a hit in the U.S. and was recently valued at over $6 billion.
Groupon, however, did not quickly enter the Middle East and local entrepreneurs seized the market. Companies such as Cobone.com (UAE), GroupIn.pk (Pakistan) and Deals.Mocality.co.uk (Kenya) used similar business models

and took a big chunk of the local market before Groupon arrived a few years later.

Similarly, eBay didn't have the marketing reach for the UAE, so Webpreneurs launched Souq.com to bring a similar business model to this part of the world. These Webpreneurs knew eBay had been successful in America and saw an opportunity to bring the future to their country.

Amazon.com, the largest seller of books in the U.S., sells more books for its electronic reader than it sells regular books. If you are in the paper or printing business, you want to assess how long it might be until "the future" arrives in your part of the world. Some technologies spread globally within a few years (Facebook, mobile phones), while others can take longer (the car, air travel). Perhaps in your part of the world, at some stage digital books will become more popular than paper books, too.

This book will help you see the future, but the past is also important. You can learn how to "stand on the shoulders of giants," that is, learn from the industry's pioneers. Skeptics in the Middle East, for example, say: "But people here don't trust the Web enough to use their credit cards online." Amazon.com overcame that objection in the 1990s. It is now a multibillion-dollar business. Some solutions will have to be localized. Online credit card use is not as widespread in the Gulf. Emiratis, for example, still like to use couriers such as Aramex and purchase using Cash on Delivery.

But people around the world are not that different from each other. You will see young people using the same mobile phones no matter where they live. This generation has a greater affinity for the world than the older generation. A teenager in Karachi can watch Justin Bieber on YouTube just like a teenager in New York. A few decades ago, pop stars would have been segmented; TV stations in Pakistan, say, would show only local TV stars.

Predicting the future will help you make career choices. If you knew that the TV was coming to your part of the world for instance, you might start a production company, an advertising company or a TV repair shop. You might choose to study mass communication in university.

You have to use your own trial and error to see what trends catch on in your part of the world. Will the Groupon or eBay business models work where you are?
You will find businesses often fail not because of the idea, but because they were not marketed effectively. People laughed when someone came up with the idea to sell bottled water. Now it is as popular in the UAE as it is in the U.S.

The world we live in now allows us to follow what is happening in other parts of the world as if we were actually living there. For instance, someone in Angola can chat with someone in California, watch Californian TV or take an online course from a California university. You might be reading about technology trends in a California newspaper and see, for instance, that Twitter is becoming extremely popular. But when you do your own survey of the Angolan market, you realize Tweeting isn't a big thing. Be careful not to base your business around a trend that hasn't made it to your area yet. You want to learn from the world but be a simple step ahead of your local market.

We can already tell you some good news from the future. Your age, qualifications and nationality won't limit you as much. It used to be that if you didn't have the right degree, you couldn't join the right company and you wouldn't get the right salary. In the Internet economy, you can short-cut your way to a profession instead of having a corporation dictate your career path. You can move at your own pace rather than society dictating your speed. This implies, of course, that it's your responsibility to take control of your education.

Being the only kid on the block with a PlayStation begins to get boring pretty quickly. You want your friends to have one, too. It makes gaming more interesting. Owning the only fax machine in the world is useless. The more people who buy a fax machine, the more useful it becomes.

Driving also improved when more people started buying automobiles. The more cars on the road, the better the roads became. More gas stations opened and car companies invested more in research and development and offered more features. Even as things improved, the price of cars came down.

In the same way, if more of us are on the Web, the better it gets for all of us. Governments start making more services available online. More companies offer their products online. Education levels improve faster the more students use the Web to learn. YouTube and Wikipedia get more people to contribute. You can even make the case that the Internet helps reduce poverty and makes the world safer. If our neighbors have something productive to do, they are less likely to steal from you.

You might be the perfect driver, but if everyone else on the road is a bad driver, you still suffer the consequences and get into accidents. This is why you want as many people as possible passing driving tests. If everyone is at a standard level of competence, we all feel safer on the road. We should encourage everyone to achieve a basic level of familiarity with the Web, so we all might benefit.

Moving Up the Innovation Curve

If you have studied marketing, you might have seen the innovation curve. In essence, any innovation usually goes through five stages:

• Innovators
• Early adopters
• Early majority
• Late majority
• Laggards

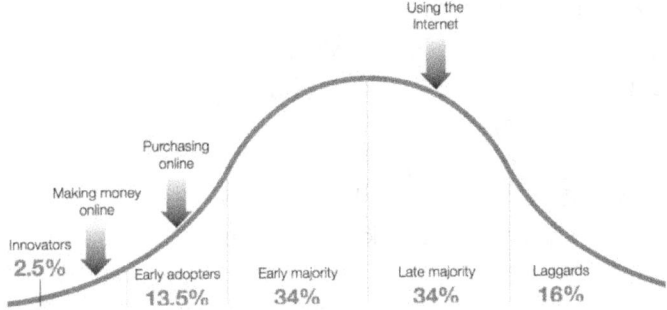

Innovators buy new products as soon as they come out. They read all the technology magazines and wait in line for the newest gizmo or gadget. Some of these technologies take off while others fail at the early stages. The BetaMax videocassette recorder, for instance, came out in the 1980s, the same time VHS was launched. Many innovators thought BetaMax was superior, but VHS prevailed. A similar competition is going on right now between DVDs, which replaced VCRs, and Blu-ray Discs, which is the newer technology.

In the mid-1990s, innovators started using the Web. By 2012, over two billion people were online, 800 million of whom use Facebook. The Internet is now in the late majority stage, especially in the U.S., where over 78% of the population access the Web.

The number of people who actually buy online is a lot lower, though this too depends on where you live. Americans, for example, spend the most money online, just as they spend the most at bricks and mortar stores. Finally, there are the few people — right now less than 1% of the two billion users — who make an income from the Web. But many people indirectly rely on the Web to help them do business. They just don't realize it until their email goes down.

Most people use the Web to:
• Check email (e.g., Hotmail, Yahoo, Gmail)
• Use a social network (e.g., Facebook)
• Search (Google)
• Check their bank account
• Watch videos (e.g., YouTube)
• Read news (e.g., bbc.co.uk, cnn.com)

That is, people are primarily consuming content or helping someone else make money. Fewer people sell their products and services through the Web.

This book will help you, if you take action, to become part of that 1%. Our goal is to encourage people to move to the right side of the innovation curve. If you are among the few who are not using the Internet yet, we encourage you to start, and if you are, we encourage you to become a Webpreneur.

The statistics on how the Internet is growing around the world are illuminating. Over 30% of the world now has access to the Internet. America has 78% penetration, while Africa lags behind with 11% penetration. But the emerging continent has the highest growth rate — 2,500% in the past decade — and the one in 10 Africans who is connected is most likely to have a disposable income.

The penetration of TV, electricity and telephones was also much higher in the U.S. and eventually spread to laggards such as Africa. This book is not a critical look at Africa; as we explained earlier, just because there is an innovation does not mean people should use it. America has one of the highest penetrations of guns in the world; that doesn't mean more guns are good for your country, too.

Mobile phone penetration is still much higher than that of the Internet, especially in the emerging world, and through cell phones, the Internet will spread even faster. Access to the Internet used to be expensive as companies had to dig holes and lay cables to order to connect homes through telephone lines. The cellular networks that connect mobile phones are much cheaper because as the signal is transmitted through the air. The same technology can now be used to provide Internet service.

Better roads, railways and communication infrastructure in the past century have helped the U.S. and Europe create a lot of wealth for its citizens. As the world goes digital, emerging countries have a great opportunity to leapfrog others if they invest in high-speed Internet connections. Looking at the growth numbers, it is not hard to convince you that the Internet is here to stay; it's just a matter of whether you will help bring the future to your part of the world, or wait for someone else to do it.

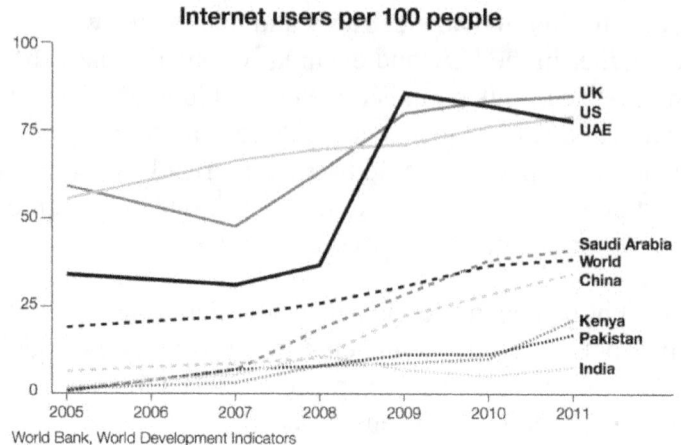

Internet users per 100 people

UK
US
UAE

Saudi Arabia
World
China

Kenya
Pakistan

India

World Bank, World Development Indicators

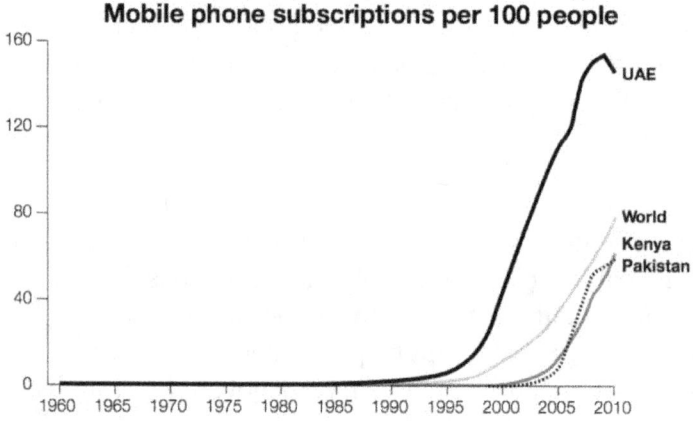

Mobile phone subscriptions per 100 people

UAE

World
Kenya
Pakistan

World Internet usage and population statistics, December 31, 2011

World region	Population, 2011 (est)	Internet users - Dec 31, 2000	Internet users - latest data	Penetration (% population)	Growth, 2000-2011	Users % of table
Africa	1,037,524,058	4,514,400	139,875,242	13.5%	2,988.4%	6.2%
Europe	816,426,346	105,096,093	500,723,686	61.3%	376.4%	22.1%
Middle East	216,258,843	3,284,800	77,020,995	35.6%	2,244.8%	3.4%
North America	347,394,870	108,096,800	273,067,546	78.6%	152.6%	12.0%
Latin America/Caribbean	597,283,165	18,068,919	235,819,740	39.5%	1,205.1%	10.4%
Oceania/Australia	35,426,995	7,620,480	23,927,457	67.5%	214.0%	1.1%
World total	6,930,055,154	360,985,492	2,267,233,742	32.7%	528.1%	100.0%

Source: internetworldstats.com

3. A BRIEF HISTORY OF MONEY

Most people want to be rich, but what exactly is money? In this chapter we will go back to the basics of wealth creation. Remember, in order to win any game, you need to understand the rules. If the game you want to play is Who Has the Highest Number in his or her Bank Account, you should understand how to achieve that number .

Let's assume that wealth means how much money you have. The more money you have, the richer you are. We know money does not buy you happiness, but we are sure you would rather be rich and unhappy than poor and unhappy.

From the Gift to the Virtual Economy

A few thousand years ago, humans lived in a gift economy. We lived in small communities and would not expect anything in return if we performed a task or gave something to someone. If you caught a fish, you would give it to your friend without expecting anything in return. This is similar to what you might still have with your immediate family; if you make your brother a meal, you do not expect him to make one in return.

As communities began to grow, more people became strangers, who were less trusted. The gift economy gave way to **bartering**. Now if you had spare fish, you could exchange them for a farmer's spare carrots.

Eventually this, too, became a hassle. If you had spare fish and needed shoes but the shoemaker didn't need fish, you would have to find a third party who had something the shoemaker needed. Complicated, right? That's why **commodity money** was introduced.

Now you could trade your fish for coins, which you could then spend on whatever you wanted. When you went to buy shoes, you would hand the shoemaker a gold coin, which he could then spend on whatever he wanted. Commodity money was usually gold, silver, copper or even barley; that is, it had value in and of itself.

If you imagine a large trade overseas, you can probably see the problem with commodity money. Who wants to haul a shipful of gold across the water? This led to the idea of **representative money**.

Representative money is the currency you are used to: the dollar, the euro, the rupee, the dirham, etc. The actual coins or banknotes are not really worth what they represent. A $100 bill is not worth $100. We as society have agreed that the note that says "$100" can be used to buy other products and services that represent $100.

In the past few decades, we have even moved on to virtual money.

Now if you want to buy something you give the shop your credit card, which tells your bank to subtract a number from your bank account and add a number to the seller's bank account. When you do an online bank transfer the same thing happens. Numbers are exchanged in databases but nothing physical moves.

You can say you are a millionaire, but it's just a number in a database. Wealth is important, but too often we let a number cause us stress. It works the other way, too. If you feel financially strapped, remember, all you have to do is to figure out how to make that number positive and as large as possible. At the end of the day, the number still represents

value; the more fish you can catch and sell, the higher the number.

4. THE SIMPLE WEALTH FORMULA

Now that we understand how the scoring works, let us simplify the formula for creating wealth:

(Amount of Value You Can Add) **x** (Number of People You Can Impact) **-** (Number of People Who Can Do What You Do) **-** (Cost to Serve) = Total Wealth Created

If you understand basic algebra, you see you want to make the top two parts of the equation as big as possible and the bottom two as low as possible. Let's look at each of the factors and see how the Internet helps you manipulate the equation.

A little disclaimer about the formula – this is meant to help you understand the bigger picture of how you can create wealth rather than a "plug and play" of numbers. Look at increasing or decreasing the factors and how it will impact your business or personal wealth rather than looking for exact values to put in.

Amount of Value You Can Add

You might tip a doorman $1 since he saved you the effort and time by opening the door for you. If you needed a heart surgeon, you would give him $10,000 (and probably whatever you had) since he could save your life.

The value provided by the heart surgeon is much greater than the value provided by the doorman, which is why a heart surgeon makes a lot more money than a doorman. There is one thing that you and Bill Gates have in common. We all have the same amount of time: 24 hours a day. But the more value you can create for each of those hours, the more wealth you will create.

The CEO of a large corporation makes over a hundred times what an average employee makes, because if the CEO helps 1,000 employees generate an extra $100 per year, the corporation makes an extra $100,000 per year. If a manager lower in the company helps all 10 of his employees make an extra $100, the company makes only $1,000 more. The value the CEO provides is much greater than that of the manager, so the CEO is compensated more.

Let's look at an example of a $20 book sold by Amazon.com. Value is created and money paid to different people in the chain:
• $20 is taken from your bank account and added to a retailer such as Amazon.com.
• $1 is given to Visa for processing the credit card transaction • $4 is given to Aramex for delivering the book
• $2 is given to the printers
• $7 is given to the publisher for marketing and distributing
• $2 is given to the author for writing the book
• $2 is given to the affiliate that helped bring the sale to Amazon
• $2 is kept as profit for Amazon

Multiple parties make money of this one transaction. Nothing material is exchanged – databases communicate with each other and transfer the appropriate amount to everyone who has provided value to you.

To make money, you have to figure out a way to **provide value to the world**. The more value you can provide, the more money you will make. We are using Microsoft Office to write this book. We paid $100 to buy a copy but feel we are getting more than $100 worth of value and so we are happy to have paid that price.

If you paid $20 for this book, you should get at least $20 worth of entertainment or education to feel good about the transaction. If you think you got fair value for this book, you are more likely to recommend it to a friend or buy our next book. If you think you overpaid, we are not likely to grow our businesses.
As long as you can create a large amount of value yet charge a lower amount for that value, you will create wealth.

Using Shovels or Teaspoons

If you are asked to dig a giant hole in the ground, do you use a teaspoon or a shovel?

The answer depends on how you are getting paid. If you are making a high hourly wage then you might as well use the teaspoon; the longer you can make the task last, the more money you make. It doesn't matter how fast you dig.

If you are an entrepreneur, chances are you are getting paid by the number of holes you dig. You want to dig as quickly as possible, so you would use a shovel rather than a teaspoon; if you could find digging equipment to do the job even faster, you would use that instead.
Remember, in most cases the world rewards you for the **value you create**, not the time you spent to create that value. For instance, do you care if this book took us a week to write or a few years to write? The output is what you are concerned with; if we could have created the same-quality book in half the time, we would have doubled our return on investment.

It is the same for most creative work. You care about the emotional impact of the movie, the quality of the song or the user-friendliness of the software, not how long it took to create.

Education can increase potential value. If you didn't know shovels existed, you would have no choice but to use a teaspoon. If someone demonstrated a shovel, you would realize the tool's dramatic effect on your hole-digging time and use it right away. You would also quickly adopt a more efficient shoveling technique if it were taught to you.

We used to have to write letters with a pen and paper. If you had a business idea and wanted to tell 10 people about it, you would need 10 hours to do the writing. If half the people who read your letter gave you $100, you would end up with $500 or $50 per hour. With word- processing software such as Microsoft Word it might still take you an hour to produce the first letter but less than a minute to print out the other nine copies. You would still make $500 but for only one hour's work. Technology and education in this example have enabled you to increase your hourly rate to $500 an hour.

It sounds basic, but this is how the wealth of nations has been created. An American farmer has agricultural machinery that allows him to do the equivalent work of a hundred farmers based in Bangladesh. The American farmer's hourly output is significantly higher.

Education in developed countries has been traditionally much better than in developing countries, so their citizens have been able to produce more per hour.

Imagine a farmer in an emerging part of the world who needs to sell his vegetables. If he doesn't have a car, it might take him two days to get his produce to market. A developed-country farmer would have a truck that would enable him to make the same journey in an hour. The value a developed-country farmer gives to the world is higher because of his superior equipment. Of course, fancy tools would be useless if the farmer didn't know how to use them. Many people have access to the Internet, but they do not know how to use it to save time or create wealth.

Perceived Value

Perceived value is also important in wealth creation. You might notice that when you buy original software, the physical disc comes in a big package. This makes consumers think they are getting more. Consumers are just beginning to appreciate the value of digital products. When you fly first-class on an airline, the airline gives you nice cutlery, dishes and better food to increase the perceived value of your experience and justify the cost, which is double or triple that of an economy ticket.
If you go to a high-end barbershop, it might offer you tea or coffee. The cost of the tea is minimal, but it improves the experience and justifies the higher price.

Impact of the Web on Value Creation

The Internet impacts your ability to create more value and hence more wealth. In the old economy, we as authors would need to find a publisher. For editing, printing and marketing our book, it would receive approximately $7 of the $20 price. If the book were sold through a traditional store in a shopping mall, a retailer would keep $7 to cover its costs (e.g., rent, salaries). In the end, we would take home only $2.

Now we can publish directly through websites such as Lulu.com and CreateSpace.com. Once we have written the book, we simply upload it and choose the Print On Demand service. When you order the book through Amazon, for example, Lulu or CreateSpace prints a single copy and ships it to you.

This drastically changes the book publishing industry. We can do the marketing and promotion ourselves, then direct our customers to order from a website, which then fills the orders. Instead of making $2, we can now take home at least $9 of the $20. In return for the bigger percentage, though, we had to create more value than the traditional publisher model. As we create more value, we make more money.

Let's say you were a journalist before the Web came along. You made a salary (usually relatively low) in exchange for the articles you wrote.

The articles appeared in a newspaper, which made money by selling advertising to accompany the articles.
In the Internet economy, you can start a blog or website and publish the same article. Instead of having an editor vet your stories or a salesperson sell advertising space, you can control more of the value chain. You can start your own free website at sites such as WordPress.com(visit www.amiranzur.wordpress.com to see an example), Tumblr.com or Blogger.com. You can now publish your article for free. You do not need to pay for an expensive printing press, a distributor to get your articles on newsstands or an advertising salesperson.
You can then sign up for an affiliate account with Amazon.com, which will give you 5-15% commission for any products you help it sell. This is an automatic deal that everyone can sign up for; you do not need an agent to convince Amazon.

If 1,000 people come to your website and read an article, perhaps 100 will click on Amazon's banner, let's say an ad for a $10 book. Of those 100, maybe 10 end up buying the book. Amazon gives you 10%, or $1 for every book it sells, which means you would make $10 for every 1,000 visitors.

The nice thing about this is you don't have to do any more work whether 100 people visit your website or a million, whether 10 books are sold or 1,000. Just the amount you make increases.

A second method to make money from your article is to sign up with Google AdSense. This is also free. Google will use a little bit of your website real estate to show ads, which it finds for you. The search engine has an automated program that determines what ads are most relevant to your content and therefore most likely to be clicked. If your website were about pets, it would display dog food ads, for example. If someone clicks on the ad, Google charges that advertiser $1, half of which it gives to you. Depending on your content, you can make a lot more than $1 per click. Advertisers for certain types of insurance and financial-based products, for instance, pay more. In effect Google is like a real estate agent in renting out your real estate space to advertisers and taking a commission.

In this scenario, you took care of advertising sales (with Amazon or Google AdSense, both of which required minimal set-up and cost nothing), printing (your free Wordpress/Tumbr/Blogger website; you can also buy your own domain by visiting HostGator.com) and distribution (people get your content on their home computers rather than having to go to a newsstand).
You can now make money directly rather than getting a job at a newspaper. Of course, this is not as easy as we make it seem; your articles have to be popular and your readership takes time to grow. But, if you have the perseverance, you can be successful.

TheHuffingtonPost.com used this model and was eventually bought out by AOL Time Warner for $315 million. Newspaper publishing is a good example of how the Internet destroyed millions of jobs (sales executives, distributors, printers) but created millions more (journalists, writers, content creators).

If you live in Ethiopia, for instance, you can publish your online newspaper and target Ethiopians living in the U.S. Even if you get just 1,000 readers from each state, you would have 50,000 customers. In the old economy this would be difficult as the cost of distributing only 1,000 newspapers would be too high. If you couldn't sell the papers, you lost money. Unencumbered by printing or distribution costs, you can quickly change your online focus, from the U.S. market to London or Tokyo, for example.

You can see how you can add a lot more value to the world via the Web. The process of printing, sales and distribution has been automated, giving you more power. All you need to focus on now is creating better content.
In many countries you needed a license to become a journalist; on the Internet you already have permission to write. You used to need a publisher to tell you your book was worth publishing; on the Internet you can post whatever you like. The only thing stopping you is your mindset. And time — there are only 24 hours in a day, even for Bill Gates.

Number of People You Can Impact

If our heart surgeon made $1,000 per operation and could treat 10 people a day, he would make $10,000. If he could help 100 people, he would make $100,000.

Bill Gates became one of the richest people in the world because his software was able to impact millions of people. The world's richest entertainer, Oprah Winfrey, had a TV show that was watched by millions.

An actor living in an African village might make a few thousand dollars in plays at the local theater. Tom Cruise might make $20 million in movies that play in cinemas around the world. Millions pay. The African actor and Tom Cruise both have to learn their lines, put in the same effort and do the same work. But Tom Cruise impacts millions and hence creates a lot more wealth.

For thousands of years, restaurateurs usually owned one or two establishments, usually in their neighborhood, where they keep an eye on them. The late Ray Kroc, who founded McDonald's, became one of the richest men in the world because he came up with systems and processes that enabled anyone in the world to run one of his restaurants. There are now over 33,000 McDonald's that employ 400,000 employees worldwide. Owning a system that facilitated over 100 billion hamburgers to be served is more lucrative than owning a small restaurant serving a few hundred local customers.

McDonald's does not own all its restaurants, but its system allows entrepreneurs to run their own restaurants using the company's brand and formula for success. Kroc made his fortune by finding a way to impact more people.

Again, we are typing this document using Microsoft Word. Microsoft spent millions to create the first version of its word-processing software. But each successive copy costs next to nothing, requiring just a click of a computer button. Yet Gates' company makes $100 for each copy of Word. Imagine how many millions of people around the world use this software. Multiply that number by $100. That's why Bill Gates is one of the richest people in the world.

One reason an average American makes $45,000 per year while an average Pakistani makes $1,000 is that American companies impact more people. America has free trade with its neighbors Canada and Mexico. Pakistan has limited trade with India, even though deregulating would give it access to a billion more customers. All 300 million Americans speak the same language, English. Multiple languages are spoken in Pakistan. America's roads, railways, airports and harbors make it easier to reach more people, quicker. Pakistan's transportation infrastructure is not as sophisticated especially to remote villages.

Americans can also travel easier, making it easier to spread their ideas and products across the globe. There might be a Pakistani Bill Gates, but he is probably stuck in a line, waiting for a travel visa.

Impact of the Web on Number of People Impacted

How can the Internet help you impact more people? Imagine you were a journalist in Johannesburg before the Web caught on. The only people who could read your articles were South Africans, and even they had to pick up the newspaper on the day your article was published. If they were out of town or too busy to read the paper that day, you got one less reader.

Now, as soon as your article is posted on the Internet, people can read it, and not just in Johannesburg. Your potential readership includes anyone with Web access, two billion rather than a few million. People don't have to read your article on the day it is published, either; they can read it any time, even in a few years, and anywhere, even on vacation. The work you did to write the article is the same, but now you have an asset that can bring in money (through online advertising) for years.

Imagine you ran a great bakery in the old economy. You would rely on word-of-mouth; that is, customers recommending your bakery to their friends. Before mobile phones and Facebook, people would keep in touch with fewer people. Now, an average Facebook user has 130 friends. If someone has a great experience in your bakery, he or she spreads the word online to hundreds or thousands of potential customers.

In the old economy, it was difficult to get a food critic to write about your bakery. A review in a newspaper or magazine would attract more customers, but the number of journalists was limited. Now you can approach one of the thousands of food bloggers to write about your bakery. The exposure should lead to more cake sales.

A local bookstore's customers are limited to those within driving distance. An online store such as Amazon can start a website and instantly start serving the millions of book lovers around the world.

There are only so many feet in a neighborhood, which used to limit a shoemaker's clientele. Plus, not everyone wanted the same shoes, so the shoemaker had to produce different styles. Companies such as Nike and Adidas made millions for their founders because they were able to make distribution deals to sell their shoes through retailers around the world. Now an entrepreneur such as Blake Mycoskie can launch www.toms.com and sell over 600,000 pairs of shoes.

It used to be that if you enjoyed a book and wanted to recommend it to your parents, you had to write a letter, buy a stamp and post it. A few days later, they would get your letter and maybe buy the book. Now you can email a hundred people at once, hit "like" on Facebook, or create a short video review, upload it to YouTube and tell the world about the book (this one, we hope). And those people in turn can email another hundred people or hit "like" on Facebook or spread the word in different ways. This is known as the viral effect. A large amount of wealth has been created by the viral effect.

The Internet gives you leverage, the ability to impact more with less. If you spend days working on a great presentation, you can now record it with a video camera and post it online. You still use PowerPoint and deliver the presentation to an audience, but with only one extra visitor, the video camera, you can reach people across the world. They can benefit from your presentation today, tomorrow or next year and you don't have to do any extra work.

What if you could hire one more salesperson? And what if that salesperson could work all day, all year? That is what the Internet does for your business; 24 hours a day, seven days a week, it sells your product and services to anyone, anywhere.

The Internet opens up trade for closed countries. Indians can hire Pakistanis online, and Pakistanis can collaborate with Indians; the governments haven't blocked IP addresses across borders — yet! Instead of lining up for a visa, the Pakistani Bill Gates can spend his time exposing his products to the world. Even the trade embargoes imposed on Iranians are easier to circumnavigate through the Internet.

The Internet breaks down political barriers and simply lets entrepreneurs create wealth as governments can't interfere with ecommerce as they do with the rest of the economy.

More trade with more people leads to greater wealth for the world.

Number of People Who Can Do What You Do

It is relatively easy to become a doorman. You can learn the job in less than an hour. To become a good heart surgeon, you need to spend years at medical school. Any heart surgeon can become a doorman, but not every doorman can become a heart surgeon.

Since heart surgeons are more rare, they can charge more for their time. Superstar singers such as Celine Dion charge over a million dollars to perform at a private party. Why? Because there is only one Celine Dion. You can play her CDs. You can even hire a Celine Dion look-alike to sing at your party, but you will not pay her nearly as much as the real Celine Dion.

This part of the formula also explains why protecting intellectual property is important for creating wealth. In the U.S., intellectual property rights are relatively strong, so when an artist records a CD, it is illegal to copy it. The singer and the record company earn revenue with every CD sold. In the emerging world, intellectual property protection is weaker. Cassette tapes, CDs and digital copies of an artist's songs are available everywhere for free. The artists do not generate any money from CD sales, so there is little incentive for them to promote their music or grow their careers. If they can't make enough money through live performances, they might have to get a regular job.

Nike doesn't sponsor many sports stars in emerging countries, because there are so many Nike knock-offs on the market. Nike doesn't profit from advertising in countries with weak intellectual property rights, and without Nike's sponsorship, athletes do not have the money to play the sports they love for a living.

In the U.S. and the U.K. over 300,000 books are published annually. Authors know they can make an income through their book sales. In many emerging countries, books are simply photocopied without recourse from the government. There is no incentive for publishers to spend time and money marketing books that can be copied for free. In developed economies you can go to jail for photocopying books without the author's permission. Authors become unique and thus can generate more wealth.

Begin Youism

There are two types of goods: commodities and brands. Gold, silver, copper and steel are examples of commodities. You don't pay much attention to brand, because the gold from one seller is the same as the other. You buy from whomever is the cheapest.

It's harder to calculate the price for a brand. Someone might pour you a drink that tastes exactly the same as Coca-Cola, but if you know it isn't the real thing, you probably won't enjoy it as much. That is why Coca-Cola's brand is worth billions of dollars. Shoes made of exactly the same quality materials but without the Nike "Swoosh" logo will sell for a lot less than branded Nikes.

Humans can also be commodities and brands. If you are a commodity, you will make a relatively low salary. You cannot be differentiated. For instance, if you work in a McDonald's, your salary will be relatively low as there are millions of other people who can do your job. McDonald's training process has made it so that most people can learn it.

On the other hand, Pablo Picasso's paintings sell for millions of dollars. Someone else could paint the same painting, using similar materials and techniques, but since it doesn't have Picasso's signature on it, it will not make anywhere near as much money. Some people might think his paintings look like children drew them, but if you gave them an original Picasso, they would probably hang it in their house and tell all their friends. That's the power of branding.

This branding is essentially what celebrities undergo.

This is why you have to become unique to create wealth. If we had sent you a one-page résumé claiming we were Internet experts, you might have put this book aside. But by writing a book and getting you to read it, we have become unique in your eyes. A book is one way for us to establish authority as leaders in the Internet economy.

You, too, can become the go-to authority in your niche. If you are in the world of fashion, you have to identify the magazines and get them to write about you. You will then be seen as unique, not just another clothing brand.

You can research blogs and books in your niche, then write your own books and use them as your "Business Card 2.0." Books can be your calling card, which you can send to potential clients. You can use your Business Card 2.0 to attract media interest. A standard business card, résumé or brochure is much easier to create, but it is not unique. Only a few people take the time to create a book.

As the world becomes more competitive, you have to differentiate yourself. A few decades ago it was difficult to compete with Nike as TV advertising was expensive. Nike's founder established a brand, and became unique and an authority on athletic shoes. Consumers trusted Nike to provide high-quality shoes, so Nike could charge a higher price than a commodity shoe company.

Water was also a commodity until companies such as Nestlé and Evian came along. Now consumers pay different prices for brands of water.

If you want to create wealth for yourself, you have to treat yourself as a brand. Do you want to be just another film director? Or do you want to build a brand like Steven Spielberg has? Think about how you can start marketing yourself, so that people trust you and your films (or products and services).

End Brandism

Branding is another reason why developed countries win and developing countries lose. If you were to put your money in a bank account, would you put it in a Swiss bank account or a Rwandan bank account? Would you buy a Swiss watch or a Vietnamese watch? The Swiss have made a name for themselves, even though not everybody Swiss is great at banking or watch making. Unfortunately, the brands of many emerging countries are not as powerful. You might be an amazing Yemeni software programmer, but since Yemen is not traditionally associated with superstar engineers, it is harder to sell yourself in the global market unless you can brand yourself better.

Like it or not, your name, gender, skin color and nationality are parts of your brand. You would have different ideas about this book if it were written by Tony Jones, Linda Jones, Tyrone Jackson, Heinz Schneider, Fatima Mohammed, Liu Chan or Deepak Patel, even if the content were the same. When we can't see people's physical appearance, we tend to stereotype them by the next best thing: their name.

You may wish to change your name for instance Andrew Warner of Mixergy.com found that his response was much better than when using Sukili Kallili as having an American sounding name got better responses. Amir Anzur also rebranded from Amir Ahmad to give a more neutral branded name.

There is also negative branding. You might set up the best eCommerce site in the world, but if you are from Nigeria, customers might not trust you. Only a handful of Nigerians might scam people on the Internet, but the impact is felt by the other 167 million. Trust in the Nigerian brand plummets, making it harder for honest Nigerians to create wealth.

Every time there is negative news about your country in the global media, it impacts your business. Consumers and employers become more cautious about doing business with people of your nationality. Terrorist attacks in Pakistan might be carried out by just a handful of people, but the headlines make it harder for the other 180 million Pakistanis to get jobs, sell products and services or travel.

In the Middle East, Dubai has been able to create a powerful positive brand. An Internet startup from Dubai is more believable than one from Yemen, because people are more familiar with Dubai than Sana'a. This makes it easier for Dubai-based companies to do business than other cities in the region.

Be aware of what the place where you live says about you to the world. Help those around you to promote a more positive image for your city or country. You might want to make negative remarks about your leaders, but you could end up hurting your brand if international customers associate your country with its politicians. Bring positive change to where you live and highlight its success, rather than just reporting bad news (which traditional media love to do to attract more viewers/readers).

You can beat brandism by letting people get to know you better. People tend to be brandist if they don't know someone. Once they get to know an individual, they tend to judge less. As you read this book, you are getting to know Talha, Mohsin and Amir Anzur, so we have already differentiated ourselves from the millions of other on the Internet.

We were able to break down stereotypes by getting you to read this book. You are now focused on our words and are less likely to care if we are short, fat, dark or white.
The great thing about the Internet is that it enables you to be judged for your work rather than your looks. In the real world people judge you on your weight or how you dress. Multinationals look at your work visa before hiring you. We call this "passportism." We have hired people online as critical parts of our team (designers, programmers, editors) without even seeing a picture of them. As entrepreneurs, we are more concerned about their output than their looks.

We stereotype to save ourselves time. It would take forever to get know a billion Chinese people, so we rely on the impressions we got from the last Chinese person we met or images we got from the media. Only if we visit the country would we be able to discover the Chinese are actually a billion individuals, not just one type.
We all stereotype because we don't have time to get to know everyone. It's a short cut, and as long as you don't box people in based on their nationality, you can use impressions to identify your expectations of someone. The point is to be aware of who you are and how others might perceive your brand.

Jobology

There was a time when you would write a one- or two-page résumé. If the employer liked your résumé, you could get a job interview, and be asked questions for an hour or so. If you passed the interview, you might be offered a job.

Through social networks such as Facebook, LinkedIn, Twitter, YouTube or your own website, you have the chance to differentiate yourself from the thousands of other people applying for the same job. Only 30% of jobs are found through advertisements or postings, which means 70% are found through networking. If you create enough of a brand for yourself, people will contact you.
Since you have more contacts through the web, your chances of hearing about a job are higher. Remember: Everything online says something about you. Like it or not, more and more employers will check your Facebook profile before hiring you. Even Facebook enables you to show off your talent.

Google receives over 20,000 résumés a week, but how many do you think are actually read? Are most of those résumés not a commodity? Building your personal online brand can make you unique so you can charge a higher amount for your services. Branding is critical to wealth creation.

If you are the best heart surgeon in the world, you will make much more money than an average heart surgeon. Specialists make more money than general practitioners because they have unique skills and are harder to find. Relatively few people may need to see a neurosurgeon, for example, but since there are so few of them, they can charge more for their services.

In London, taxi drivers known as black cabs make over $80,000 per year. The reason for their relatively high income? The city has a quota on the number of black-cab licenses. Since the supply is limited, these drivers charge more.

A security guard working in New York can make $2,000 per month. The same guard with the same skills in Nepal could make only $100 per month. In the old economy, the New York guard's passport made him unique. If there were a true free economy, many Nepalese security guards would move to New York, driving salaries down to maybe $1,000 per month. But the U.S. government legislated that anyone working in their country has to make at least $7 per hour and pay taxes. They also controlled immigration so the New York security guard could keep his higher salary without fear of competition. Companies might have wanted to hire Nepalese guards, but since they didn't have U.S. work visas they couldn't.

Most online jobs are not limited by work visas. The uniqueness that came from simply being born in the right place is gone. People get jobs only if they deserve them. If you asked us as entrepreneurs to choose between a book-cover designer based in New York who charged $1,000 or one based in Dhaka, Bangladesh who charged $100, we would, of course, choose the Bangladeshi, especially if his or her work was the same. Humans came up with the concepts of countries and segmentation; the Earth wasn't created that way. The Internet is breaking down those barriers.

Adam Smith, one of the fathers of modern economics, wrote *The Wealth of Nations* in the 1700s. He believed the division of labor or specialization was the key to creating wealth. The Internet allows you to specialize. You might be the best shoelace designer, but if there is no demand in your village, you can't make a living doing what you love. With the Internet, if you can brand yourself as "The greatest shoe lace designer in the world," you can create wealth. This specialization will attract a shoelace factory somewhere else that desperately wants to work with the greatest shoelace designer in the world.

If all of us have the same skills, the income we can earn will be limited. If we all have unique skills, the wealth we can create will be greater. On our team, for example, we might hire someone to video edit, another to write the book, another to market it and another to create a website. If all four were video editors, there would have no need for three of them, so we would just hire the cheapest.

Cost to Serve

McDonald's became profitable because its food service processes allowed it to get more output per employee than its competitors. One employee could serve 100 customers in the time a competitor could deal with only 70. In the fast-food industry, labor is 70% of the cost, meaning McDonald's had more than a 40% lower cost-to serve.

Facebook has become one of the most valuable companies in the world because its costs to serve are lower. Compare Facebook to a magazine. Both business models are built around advertising to readers.
Journalists write articles for a magazine, photographers take pictures, and editors put the content together. Then there are advertising salespeople and printing costs. Distributors get paid to take the magazines to the newsstands, cashiers to sell them.

Facebook gets people like you to provide status updates and pictures for free. You are journalist, photographer and editor, but you are not even getting paid for it! There are no costs to print Facebook and content storage costs are getting cheaper every year, dropping by half every two years. Advertisers don't need salespeople to convince them of the right place for their ads. The segmentation of the market users wants to aim for is up to them.

Instead of translating the magazine into several languages, users automatically update their statuses in their own language; the Portuguese see content in Portuguese, the French see it in French, and the Arabs sees it in Arabic. Facebook can do all this with fewer than 3,000 employees. All that content for over 800 million people, updated 24 hours a day, 365 days a year. In the native tongue. No TV station, newspaper or radio station has even a tenth of Facebook's audience, yet employ many times the number of staff.

This self-service model has benefited many companies. Take a bank, for instance. A few decades ago the only way to check your bank balance was to go to a cashier. The advent of automatic teller machines (ATMs) meant the bank did not need to employ as many cashiers. ATMs still need to be installed and maintained in many locations, though. With the Internet, people can serve themselves. The bank saves a lot of money since it doesn't need to pay cashiers. There is less demand for ATMs since you can access your account from your home computers.

The same goes for travel arrangements. You enter your name, address and credit card number and select a flight. You don't need an agent to do this. This saves the airlines the cost to serve you. They can keep this money as additional profit or pass on savings to their customers. The consumer gets lower costs, less chance of error and much quicker service, which is available 24 hours a day, seven days a week, from anywhere.

Online retailers have also lowered their costs to serve. In the traditional economy, building a bookstore in a shopping mall cost a lot of money. Then you had to pay rent and electricity and hire staff. You probably lost a lot of money through theft, too, and 70% of that came from your own employees. Amazon can serve its customers from one large warehouse in a remote area with cheaper rent and less staff. The savings are passed on to customers.

The Internet also lowers the costs to employ people. For instance, if you lived in the UAE pre-Internet and wanted to hire a video editor, you would need to search the Subcontinent, pay for candidates' flights, obtain their work visas and provide them with accommodation. Then, and only then, could they get to work on your video. Now you can go to websites such as oDesk.com or eLance.com and hire people directly. If you live in a town with a few thousand people, it would be difficult to find an amazing software programmer, especially one willing to work for a minimal wage. Now, you can easily find great talent in a different part of the world.

To review: the population of Switzerland is 8 million. A haircut there costs $45. The population of Pakistan is 180 million. A haircut there costs $1. The Swiss education system is much better than Pakistan's, and a few decades ago this would have been a huge advantage for, say, a computer programmer. But now, Pakistanis can access MIT's website (www.mit. edu), get all the university's lectures for free, and learn to code. If they need to get their math up to snuff, they can visit www.KhanAcademy. org and get lessons from kindergarten through Grade 12 for free. A Swiss software company can choose prospective employees from Pakistan, India, the Philippines, Kenya or Egypt at a fraction of the cost. You can educate them and have them working at the productivity of a local in no time.

Then you can pass on the savings to your customers or increase your profit margins.

Nike's founder, Phil Knight, is a billionaire because he was able to get Americans to perform high-value work (creating ads, sponsoring Tiger Woods and Michael Jordan) while having low-level work (stitching shoes) done in places such as Indonesia and Vietnam. The consumer got a great product at a reasonable price and so the cost to serve was lowered. You can apply the lessons of Nike to your own cost cutting, by hiring some talent locally and some from a different part of the world. For instance, Indians might want to hire American voice-over talent so their videos sound more professional, while Americans might want to hire data-entry operators from India.

As the world becomes more globalized, many talented people in emerging countries will make far more than untalented people in developed countries. The talent, and the marketing of that talent, rather than the color of one's passport will be the key to wealth creation.
Business can happen only once trust is established between two people. Before the Internet, it took time to get to know strangers and establish trust.

In the book *Three Cups of Tea*, author Greg Mortenson quotes a village chief in Pakistan:

"Here [in Pakistan and Afghanistan], we drink three cups of tea to do business; the first you are a stranger, the second you become a friend, and the third, you join our family, and for our family we are prepared to do anything – even die."
    Haji Ali, Korphe village chief, Karakoram Mountains, Pakistan

The Internet enables you to do business by drinking two cups of tea instead of three. People can learn about you by researching you online. You don't have to repeat yourself; once you start increasing your Web presence, people across the world will feel they know you. This ultimately saves you time, as trust is instantly established so business can happen quicker.

This book for us is like having a cup of tea with you. Once you read it, you feel you can trust us. We don't have to spend as much time getting to know each other, which means less time with lawyers and more time doing business.

More and more people work as freelance agents now. Developing relationships cost these people time, which is, of course, a cost. Once a freelancer's brands is established on the Internet, the time he or she needs to start business relationships decreases, saving everyone involved money.

Summary of the Simple Wealth Formula

Let's revisit the Simple Wealth Formula:
>   Amount of Value You Can Add
>   **x** Number of People You Can Impact
>   - Number of People Who Can Do What You Do
>   - Cost to Serve
>   = Total Wealth Created

You can see how simple wealth creation is. You create value for the world by doing what you do best (hairstyling, graphic design, computer programming, making hamburgers, entertaining or educating). The Internet gives you more tools to do things yourself or connect with people who can help you.

You have to appeal to as many people as possible, and thanks to the Internet, two of the seven billion people on the planet world are connected. You need to be unique, to differentiate yourself from the other seven billion. And through the Web you have more opportunities to find your niche and establish relationships. There might be others who can do your job as good, if not better, but you can create a brand that people trust and want to be associated with.

Great brands such as Louis Vuitton, Nike and Rolex took decades to create, and you, too, will have to think of the long term. Connect with your fellow students while you are still in school, as they are your customers, suppliers or business partners of the near future. A brand is created one person at a time, and your friends see you as a brand, too.

Finally, look to decrease your cost to serve. You do not have to buy everything locally because there is great talent around the world available to help you at the click of a mouse. There are also many tools on the Internet that can drastically save you time and money.

5. FOUR TYPES OF WEALTH CREATORS

In the book *Rich Dad, Poor Dad*, authors Robert Kiyosaki and Sharon Lechtor talk about the four types of wealth creators:

1. **Employee** – these people have a standard salary and a job working for someone else.

2. **Self-Employed** – these are the doctors or lawyers who run their own practice. But if they are ever ill or don't turn up to work, they don't make money.

3. **Business Owners** – these are the people such as Bill Gates and Steve Jobs who create their own businesses.

4 **Investors** – these are people such as Warren Buffet who have money work for them by purchasing a stake in other businesses.

You can create wealth no matter what category you are in, but some have more limitations. If you are already on a career path, determine who the richest employee is and how much money you could make in that job. You will find there is usually a limit to what you can earn. Being an employee has many benefits, not least of which is a stable income every month. If you love what you do, being an employee is a good category to be in.

Self-employed people love the freedom of being their own boss. They can choose the hours they work and the activities they want to do. The only problem with most self-employed people or freelancers is that they have limited ability to scale. Again, if they are ill, they are not likely to earn money. If they want to double their income, they need to work double the hours or double their rates.

Business owners can start to scale their products and services. Ray Kroc, the McDonald's founder, was not the hamburger chef at his restaurant. Instead he created the **systems and processes** that allowed his hamburgers to be served around the world. He made a little bit from each hamburger sold. This category is where the likes of Richard Branson, Steve Jobs and Bill Gates fall into.
Investors have their money work for them. For instance, they give a startup $10,000 for a 20% stake in the company.

The Internet helps all groups. Employees can find better jobs by searching sites such as LinkedIn to see who works at the company they want to work at, connect with them and send in their résumé.

The self-employed have better marketing opportunities. Using sites such as Facebook, the self-employed can make sure they are not forgotten. If you are friends with your dentist and every time you log in to your Facebook account you see his or her dental tip, you are not likely to forget the person for your next visit. For the self-employed, it is important to be seen as an authority in their niche. Would you go to the average dentist or the best dentist you could afford?

The self-employed can attract more customers by providing free educational content. A dentist can set up a system that shows a weekly three-minute video on how to take care of your teeth. Although the dentist is giving free advice, it is really a form of marketing. Customers are more likely to visit a dentist they know and trust and more likely to recommend him or her to their friends. The video helps build the dentist's clientele.

Business owners primarily use the Web to market their company. They also use the Web to hire and train their employees, reducing costs by hiring globally or using software to manage more and more of their business, allowing them to create systems and processes so customers do more of the work themselves (e.g., booking an airline ticket online rather than through an agent) and monitor employees (e.g., monitoring sales performance through tools such as Salesforce.com).

People who might not have had a chance to invest a few decades ago can now afford to. To buy a McDonald's franchise costs anywhere from $500,000 to $1 million. Then you have to rent space, hire staff and buy furniture. Now you can start an online business with a few hundred dollars. If you live in a richer part of the world, you might invest in a startup in a poorer part of the world because of the price difference.
When your idea begins to work, you can then scale it to a richer part of the world.

This is where a big shift in the economy is happening. People with safe jobs making a decent living are investing in ventures around the world. In the old economy, people such as Warren Buffet would buy shares in publicly traded companies on the New York Stock Exchange. He influenced decisions and made a profit if they grew.

You, too, can now search out entrepreneurs in a different part of the world, invest money and take a stake in the company. Once the idea proves itself in one niche it can grow. If you are looking for investors, you need to create a Web presence to convince potential partners. People do not like to invest in strangers, but they will invest in entrepreneurs they believe in. Instead of investing $10,000 in a huge company such as Google or General Electric in which they have no control over the direction of the company, they can invest $10,000 in a smaller company and have more input.

Companies have become cheaper and cheaper to start, making it possible for more and more ordinary people to invest. The returns can be huge but the company can take years to get off the ground. The Internet enables more people to become investors or business owners, which is where true wealth is possible. The collaboration of developing-world entrepreneurs and developed-world part-time investors is going to be a bigger trend. More regular employees in developed-world countries will set aside $500 to $1,000 per month to hire intelligent, driven entrepreneurs in developed countries to produce products and services for their part of the world.

An easy way to start a business is to look for a problem to solve. What software or service could solve a problem in your part of the world? If you have a few hundred dollars to spare, you can hire and train someone from an emerging country to work on your problem. It's usually more fun to have a stake in a startup than a boring bank account accruing less than 5% interest.

6. HOW TO CLONE YOURSELF

A few thousand years ago if you discovered how to start a fire you would call people around you and demonstrate it live. This limited the number of people you could tell about your new knowledge since you would always have to be there. There was only one of you, so you were limited to the places that you could travel. Knowledge tended to stay local.

A few hundred years later, humans discovered how to draw. You could now create cave drawings to show others how to start a fire. You didn't have to be there; you had effectively cloned yourself. People could come to your cave at their own convenience and get instructions on how to start a fire. Your cave drawings taught, even when you were not there.

Eventually we discovered pen and paper and could handwrite instructions and communicate discoveries to different parts of the world. Writing by hand was a slow process, but Johannes Guttenberg made it cheaper and more accessible in the 1440s when he invented the printing press. Now you could write your instructions once, and millions could receive your knowledge.

The radio came along in the early 1900s, and your message could now be broadcast to millions, who could listen while they went about their daily chores.

By the 1930s, TV was invented and now you could give a live demonstration of how to start a fire. People could actually see you. An even better clone had been created.

The printing press was relatively local. There was a cost associated with printing so you would need to ensure there was enough of a need before you went to press. While you could now send your message to more people, you still had to pay distribution costs.

Radio and TV stations also had costs. There was the cost of recording and the cost to transmit the signal across the country. There were only a limited number of licenses given, and since governments meted them out, you had to be careful what you said.

Few TV, radio stations or newspapers were truly global. If you were Nigerian and living in South Africa, it was unlikely you could listen to your favorite Nigerian radio station. If you could not be at home at 9 p.m. to watch your favorite TV show, that was it. Unless you had someone to record it for you the show was gone forever.

By the mid-1990s, the Internet became available to the general public. It was a combination of the printing press, radio and TV, and, even better, you could communicate with it. You could type your fire demonstration into a word processor, download it on a podcast for people to listen to in their cars, or videotape and upload it to YouTube. If your audience got confused at any time, they could email you or leave a comment on YouTube.

Your cave could be anywhere in the world, and you could communicate with anyone. Advancements in technology effectively allowed you to clone yourself.
Printing presses and radio and TV stations have gatekeepers. Resources are limited; there are only so many pages in a newspaper. Only one radio or TV show can be broadcast at a time. The gatekeepers — newspaper editors and radio and TV programmers — decided who was good

enough to go on air and the content that would appeal to readers, listeners or viewers.

If the editor of a newspaper didn't think your ability to start a fire was a story worth printing, there was little hope of you getting your idea across to the world. If a publisher didn't feel your book was any good, it wouldn't get printed and your ideas could not spread.

When the Internet came, space and time scarcities were erased. Now there was unlimited room to print your story (over 200 million blog posts are written every day). A site such as YouTube allows anyone to post almost any content (over 36 hours of video are posted every minute).

You no longer have to pitch to the gatekeepers, but can go straight to your audience. Most big media stars used to live in places such as Hollywood or New York City, since the gatekeepers lived there.

Salespeople realize how important relationships are. The more people, who know, like and trust you, the more you are likely to sell. In the old economy you would make relationships one at a time. In the Internet age, though, you can clone yourself. You can update all your friends at once on where you are and what you are doing on Facebook. In the old economy, you limited your friends since you didn't have time to keep up with too many. With more friends online, you can educate them on your products and services.

In essence, convincing people to buy is about educating them about your product's or service's benefits. Many of you who read this book, for instance, will become more interested in the web and take a WebpreneurAcademy.com course to learn more.

Steve Jobs cloned himself by launching new products on multiple platforms. Many who watched his demonstrations on their computer screens went out and bought the product. The only problem with cloning is that most of us never took media-training classes. Until a decade ago, you never had to appear in photos or on TV unless you really wanted to. Now, almost anywhere you go, someone has a phone camera and can post a picture of you on Facebook.

Let's say you wanted to learn basic trigonometry pre-Internet. If you were lucky and had a good teacher, a small enough classroom and enough confidence, you could ask your teacher about concepts you didn't understand.

If you had a lousy teacher, a huge classroom or lacked confidence, you lost out. You would fall behind in trigonometry, which would have an impact on your next class and the class after that. You might begin to feel stupid, your confidence would be shot and you would fall even farther behind.

Teachers have been able to clone themselves and spread their knowledge using the Internet. Sal Khan founded KhanAcademy.org after his nephews wanted some extra math tutoring. He wasn't in the same city, so he recorded a few lessons and sent them the link to YouTube. Before long, other kids started watching the lessons, and Khan went on to record over 2,000 video lectures covering everything from kindergarten to Grade 12. Kids can watch the lessons at their own pace, and replay them until they understand the concepts. They can visit forums, ask questions and get even more help.

The rate of innovation will get even faster. A few thousand years ago before cavemen figured out how to spread their ideas, the innovations would be local. As society progressed, people could connect, but their messages were still filtered by gatekeepers. Now people across the world can share their knowledge and build on others' knowledge so that everyone can innovate.

As we read in the chapter for wealth creation, more knowledge can lead to more value and more wealth. Someone who is educated is likely to be a user of shovels rather than teaspoons. Education used to be formal, take place in schools and depended on exams. In the Internet economy, you can learn from millions of teachers online without having to take an exam or go to school.

The quality of teachers has improved, too, since the best can clone. At the moment, most lessons are in English, but as more people come online from other countries, they will be more content in Swahili, Arabic, Korean, Hindi and Urdu. If you want to truly help your community, you, too, will need to become a Sal Khan or an Amir Anzur. Instead of teaching a few kids in a classroom, you can reach millions from your home.

Amir, for instance, runs classes online. He has researched wealth- creation content over the past few years that he believes every teenager and adult should understand. He also has live sessions in which students from places such as Singapore, New York, London, Delhi, Abu Dhabi, Sydney and Tokyo ask him questions on launching their businesses. Students can all look at the same website at the same time, something that was not possible more than a decade ago.

This ability to clone themselves across the world in the new economy will create a lot of wealth for not only salespeople, but also for teachers who would have been able to work with a limited number of students in the past.

7. LESSONS IN WEALTH FROM PRE-INTERNET AGE

They say history repeats itself, so what are the lessons we can learn from people who created great wealth in the past century? In this chapter we list some wealth creators. If you have not heard of these people or companies, we recommend you familiarize yourself with them; obviously the Internet makes it easier for you to research!

Oprah Winfrey

Oprah Winfrey became a billionaire and one of the highest-paid entertainers of the last century, building a brand that many knew, like and trusted. If Oprah lost all her money today, she could become a millionaire again almost overnight. She could partner with almost anyone to promote a product and get a share of the revenues.
If Oprah were to approach us and offer to promote this book in exchange for half the proceeds, we would gladly agree, because any book Oprah promotes makes it onto the best-seller list within a few weeks. She could have the same deal with other producers.

You can become the new Oprah Winfrey. A Chicago TV station gave her the chance to communicate through her talk show. You have YouTube, and do not need anybody's permission to start your own show. YouTube actually has a bigger global reach than any TV station that Oprah was on when she started her career.

You do not have to be living in Chicago or Los Angeles to connect with big celebrities. You can sign up for Skype and start contacting celebrities in your niche. If you have a large following or are good at interviewing, many will be happy to talk to you. You can record the conversation and upload it to YouTube. Skype is free. Connecting to celebrities is free. YouTube is free.

Interviewing authors (usually looking to promote their books) or businesspeople (looking for promote their businesses) not only gives you great content, but also is a great way to learn from the best. Over time, you will build up a network of influential people.

Building a following takes time, which you have. Oprah did her show for 25 years to build up her loyal following. You need to start somewhere, but within a few years you will have built up a following, which will result in wealth. When you build a following, you become much more important to society. Oprah has probably had more influence on American culture and society than most presidents who served during that time.

We often get approached with free products, services and even sponsorships, just to promote things to our followers. Once you become a person of influence, more and more people will ask you to help promote their products and services. Oprah did not become famous overnight. Many people start on the Internet, don't see immediate results, and give up. Creating wealth on the Internet is a marathon, with many sprints in the middle. If you want to be in this game be prepared for the long term.

How TV Created Wealth

Think of an actor working a few hundred years ago – before TV came along, the Tom Cruise of the 1800s. The only way for the old Tom Cruise to make more money would be to perform to a packed house every night.

There were three problems with this business model. First, the old Tom Cruise would have to continually perform if he wanted to make money. If he ever fell ill or wanted to take a day off, he could not make money.

Old Tom's target market was limited. He would work on Broadway, so his audience was limited to the couple of thousand New Yorkers who could fill the theater. If he wanted more people to see him perform he would have to tour different cities, and since those people hadn't seen him before, he would have to build his brand from scratch each time.

The old Tom would be stuck doing the same thing over and over again. If he wanted to work on another play, someone else would perform his old role — and make money doing it.

Thanks to TV and cinema, the Tom Cruise of the 1980s had a much easier time creating his wealth. All he had to do was act once. He could work on every scene until he got it just right. And then relax. If he fell ill or took a few days off, *Top Gun* could still be seen around the world. All he had to do is visit a few TV shows to help promote his movies. When he started working on his next movie, the old ones still made money for him.

Oprah Winfrey, Jerry Springer, Steven Spielberg, the cast of *Friends* and a whole lot of other celebrities have TV to thank for helping them create vast fortunes.

The Internet will amplify the effect of TV. Now you don't need to be based in Hollywood to be able to clone yourself. People can produce content that can be seen everywhere and forever. Your movie can be seen at any time, rather than the times set by a TV network or film distributors. Revenues models are changing so that you can make money from advertising or charge people to watch online.

Creative people around the world have a greater opportunity than at any time in history to make money, thanks to the Internet. The number of millionaires that TV generated will be a mere fraction of the number the Internet creates over the next few decades. But you will need to be creative, not only with your filmmaking or songwriting, but also with your business model.

You don't even need a broadcasting license to start your own TV channel. The Tom Cruises of the world will have a lot of competition from "nobodies" like you and us over the next few decades.

It is easier to learn the impact of a new technology by seeing how a similar technology impacted history. Knowing about a change that is coming, and taking advantage of it, however, are two different things.

How McDonald's Created Wealth

With over $24 billion of sales per year and 400,000 employees serving over 33,000 restaurants worldwide, McDonald's has become one of the most successful companies. It generated wealth by creating a system that looked beyond an individual restaurant. You can pay McDonald's to franchise its name and it will give you a system for picking a location, training your employees and serving food.

Wealth creation is about creating systems. As you build your business in the Internet economy, how can you build systems so your business can grow? The Internet allows you to systemize things so you don't need to always be there. For instance, Webpreneur Academy is our teaching system. Teachers in the old economy make much less money because they are not scaling their knowledge; they always have to be in their classrooms.

Lessons from America

The U.S. is the wealthiest country in the world. One in four dollars spent around the world is done so by an American. We are not suggesting everyone follow the country's business model, but examine some of the factors that enabled it to succeed.

One of the keys to success is great communication infrastructure. The U.S. built roads, railways and airports as well as TV and radio stations. If you were an entrepreneur and had an idea, you had plenty of methods to spread your word. One of the reasons the top Internet companies (Yahoo, Google, Facebook, eBay, etc.) are all based in California is the amount of media coverage there. *The Social Network* generated millions of dollars of publicity for Facebook, for example. Many Hollywood movies show an Apple in the background, which familiarizes audiences with the computer and helps the company gain market share. America has a culture of cross-promotion.

Notice, for instance, magazines such as *Time* and *Newsweek* often mention Apple or Microsoft in their stories. If you are based in a country such as Afghanistan, you do not have many newspapers or websites, so there are fewer people communicating about your product. Abdulla the Afghan might have created Facebook before Mark Zuckerberg came up with the idea, but Zuckerberg had the benefit of the U.S. media, which spread the word about his product. Abdulla could share his with only a few dozen of his (non-influential) friends.

The U.S. is also diverse. You might be roommates with an Italian- American or go to school with an African-

American or date an Arab-American. Diversity leads to many different points of view, which leads to innovation. American culture is also less risk-averse. In many Arab countries, for instance, people have to be careful what our family thinks. They must consider their family's honor before we do anything too drastic. In the U.S., this is less the case. Michael Jackson got more publicity for his odd behavior than a "normal" person would. The publicity helped him sell records and become more famous. Americans take more risks and come up with crazy products and services – some work and many don't. Failure is accepted as a process of innovation.

America also has a large population that speaks the same language. If you have a cool idea, it can spread quickly to 300 million people. Every town has multiple McDonald's, Wal-Marts, Starbucks and other franchises. Coca-Cola sells to McDonald's, which is available across the U.S.

Telecommunication was relatively cheap in America. Long-distance calls were cheaper than in other countries, which made it easier to do business domestically and internationally. Travel was also cheap and the workforce very mobile. It was not a problem to move from New York City to Los Angeles if someone had a better job opportunity. People in emerging countries often think more about leaving their families to settle in a different city, even if it's in their own country.

The rest of the world now has many of the advantages the U.S. had a few decades ago thanks to the Internet. If you wanted to become an author in Oman, for instance, you had an audience of three million, at most. Now, you can sell to over 350 million Arab speakers through the Web. Phones are much cheaper, and in many cases free (e.g., Skype, GoogleTalk, providing they are not banned in your country). A call from Pakistan to the U.S., for example, cost approximately $2 a minute in 1990; now it's about two cents. This means more business communication costs are lower.

Sending email is free. Compare that to the cost of a stamp to send a letter from Oman to Jordan. Now everyone can access any market from where they are. No barriers exist.

Education in America was superior to that of many other countries. The "brain drain" occurred as the brightest and most talented in the world were recruited by Harvard, Yale, and Stanford. Thousands of other universities gave their graduates a head start in life because they had the smartest professors. Now, teachers and thought leaders have their own blogs and websites and give presentations at events that are captured on camera and uploaded to YouTube. You do not have to physically attend the greatest universities to get the knowledge you want access to. Professors can build on each other's knowledge online from where they are, rather than having to emigrate.

We also can learn from negatives of the U.S. economy. There is a constant need to get more in American culture. More marketing, for instance, means a new computer game or must-have gadget comes out every few months. The constant need for new products creates wealth but sometimes at the expense of other aspects of life.

In a society that is too money-driven, family time shrinks, because it does not produce as much wealth as office time. We have to be sure to measure other meaningful assets. A home-cooked meal, for example, takes longer, costs less and generates less wealth than a meal at McDonald's. Drinking tap water does not produce as much wealth as Coca-Cola. But they are healthier, which is important in the long term. Your country probably doesn't want to follow

America's example when it comes to health: Remember, 30% of its population is overweight.

Emotional wealth is important, too. Even if you have a big number in your bank account, if you are unhealthy you won't be able to enjoy it. A New York investment banker might earn more than a street vendor in Damascus, but he is also likely to have less time to himself.

8. WEBONOMICS: BUSINESS MODELS FOR CREATING WEALTH ONLINE

The Internet is a blank canvas. You can paint any picture you want with it. There are thousands of ways to create wealth online, and in this chapter we look at a few of these opportunities.

Marketing

In essence, the Internet is a marketing tool – just like TV, radio, billboards or direct mail. You still need to have a product or a service to sell, but the Internet enables you to attract customers from across the world you might not have had access to.
Business owners want more customers, so if you tell them how you can attract more they are likely to listen.

Take, for instance, a company manufacturing air conditioners. You might propose a deal that for every air conditioner you help sell, you make $100. You would start a website — www.YouAirConditioners.com — market it, then send the manufacturer the orders you get. You get $100 for each sale.

You can also market yourself through YouTube, LinkedIn or even Facebook to get more customers for your services. If you are one of the best graphic designers in the world, for example, you can make money doing it.

Become an expert at Google Adwords or Facebook advertising and promote yourself — from anywhere in the world. Once you learn how to use the Internet as a marketing tool, many companies will pay you for your services.

You can do this on a retainer basis; that is, a company pays you a monthly fee to help it manage its social media and bring in new customers, or by commission, which a company pays you for each new order. The Internet makes it easy to track sales, so it is easier for business owners to pay marketers only for successes.

Affiliate Marketing

You do not need to get anyone to hire you to be an affiliate marketer. Many businesses use affiliates to help them sell. You can sign up free to work for a company such as Amazon (affiliate-program.amazon.com).

Here's how this works: Visitors to your website see an ad for Amazon, for instance. When they click, they are directed to Amazon's Web site and offered a promotion. If the viewer buys a book, you get a commission, up to 15% of the sale price. Amazon does not pay you for click-throughs that do not end up in sales. If a customer buys, you win and the company wins.

This method gives you incentive to create a themed website. You could launch BookReviews.com, for example, and offer links to Amazon for every book you review. It will give you an affiliate code, which lets it know the customer came from your website.

What if a customer clicks through to Amazon, but buys the book a week later? Many programs have a "cookie," which is left on the computer of the potential customer. There are 30-day, 90-day and 365-day cookies, so if the consumer purchases the product within the cookie's timeframe, you still get credit for the sale.

Websites such as ClickBank.com offer up to 75% commissions to affiliates.

The reason they can offer such high commissions is because the delivery costs of most digital products — eBooks, training courses, etc. — is almost zero. The only cost to them is a 5% credit card charge, so even if a company gives you 75% commission it still makes a 20% profit. Sellers of digital products know they can upsell; that is, offer their customers other products and services in the future. Even if they lose a little on the affiliate sale, they will profit in the future.

Amazon has over 100,000 affiliates. ClickBank.com has paid its affiliates commissions over $2 billion (that's "billion," with a "b"!). Commission Junction (CJ.com) is an affiliate management program that connects you to hundreds of companies that will pay you to help sell their products.

The great thing is that these are free to join and give you a way to start earning without have a product or relationships with any companies.

You can also join Webpreneur Academy's affiliate program – if you promote the course to your friends or others who might be interested, you make a percentage or the sales.

eCommerce

You can also start online by selling your own products, be they books, DVDs or clothes.

Payment options for your customers can include credit cards or Cash on Delivery. If you sign up with a company such as www.2Checkout.com, it will process credit cards on your behalf, even if you live in countries such as Nigeria, Pakistan, India or the UAE. You can also pay companies such as Aramex to collect cash on your behalf.

PayPal is a popular method of payment in the U.S. but is restricted in many countries. Check its website to see if it is available in your country. To create your online store you can use software such as 1ShoppingCart, InfusionSoft, OSCommerce, Shopify or ShopMarkaz. Sourcing your product is important. Websites such as www.alibaba.com will connect you to thousands of suppliers around the world that can produce products for you.

You will also need to sort out how to ship your products. FedEx, DHL, Aramex and a host of local couriers can do this for you.

Software

The best way to make money is by solving problems. What can you do to solve an issue and promote your solution? These are some examples of software ideas and companies that have been successful in that field:
• helping people manage their accounting (e.g., Quickbooks)
• helping small business manage their customers (e.g., Salesforce.com, Zoho.com)
• helping people manage their email marketing (e.g., MailChimp, aWeber, iContact, ConstantContact)
• hosting software (e.g., HostGator.com)
• eCommerce software (e.g., Shopify, ShopMarkaz.com)

There are thousands of niches (e.g., medical software) in which you can create a computer-based solution to a problem.
The more people online, the more who will be looking for software.

Sometimes software exists but is not localized. We knew of the capabilities of InfusionSoft, for example, but noticed it was marketed to U.S. customers rather than those in places such as Pakistan, Kenya and the UAE. We created ShopMarkaz as niche software for these emerging countries. Also as InfusionSoft was priced at $300 per month we knew that the business owners in the emerging world were likely to not want to pay nearly as much for the use of the software, so we lowered our pricing significantly to cater to our markets.

Localized software is a growth market. U.S. companies are unlikely to compete with you, and you can already see what worked there. You can customize the software, provide support in your local language and get local newspapers and TV to promote you. If you can create the best software in one country, it should work in many.
The software business model, known as Software As A Service or SAAS, is similar to the one for mobile phones. A customer signs up with a provider, and every month pays a phone bill, let's say $20 a month. If a telecommunications company can get 1,000 customers, it will make $20 x 1,000 = $20,000 per month.

When people sign up for SAAS, they rarely leave, especially if the software does what it is supposed to do. Provide more value than your customer pays for and you will continue to grow your business. Even though we localized when we created ShopMarkaz, you can target Europe or the U.S. without taking on any local customers.

Like Google, you can also give out the software for free and make money through advertising. You might take a loss when only three or four people use your software, but as you start to succeed and attract hundreds of customers, you will see your investment pay off.

Education

Another growth sector online is teaching. As people mature, they spend less on cars, watches and handbags and more on self-fulfillment. There are five knowledge niches people pay for:
• Business and make-money
• Health, fitness and weight loss
• Relationships and dating
• Irrational passion
• Formal education

The business and make-money niche is what entrepreneurs like to spend money on. Webpreneur Academy, for example, helps those who want to create a living for themselves. This book also falls into this category.

Health, fitness and weight loss feature products such as acne, abs- building programs and disease cures.
Relationships and dating feature products such as divorce kits and advice for finding the right partner.
Irrational passions feature products that cater to activities such as golf or stamp collecting. Avid golfers will pay for tips on achieving the perfect swing. Formal education features products that help students get into college or degree programs. People pay to improve their GMAT or SAT scores or to get their teaching or MBA degrees online.

Another great example in this category is edx.org. This website offers free online courses on almost all the subjects. The best thing is that the courses offered are designed and taught by the professors of renowned colleges and universities around the world. To add the knowledge you gain on your resume, you may get a recognized certificate after paying an economical price. There are many success stories of people who got employed by companies such as Google by just achieving valuable qualifications and skills from edx!

Services (Freelancing)

There are thousands of jobs you can do online by joining services such as oDesk.com or eLance.com and selling your talent, whether it's translation, graphic design, video editing, software programming, voice- over talent or copywriting.

If you remember the Simple Wealth Formula you know you need to differentiate yourself from the thousands of others selling their services. Some copywriters charge $10,000 for a day of their time, others do it for $5 per hour. Your rate depends on how much your customers are willing to pay. If you do not build your personal brand, employers will simply hire the cheapest workers.
Once you build your brand, the employer can justify paying you $100 an hour since it knows you are the best in your field. To make $100 per hour, you would need to target richer employers and have more valuable skills.

For most people, the best way to step into the market as a freelance service provider is by building a good profile on bidding sites such as Upwork, Guru, Freelancer etc. Such websites act as comprehensive platforms to get connected with potential clients, gain valuable experience and lay the foundations of your brand. As you become more confident, you may build your own website/blog and seek professional relations with the experts of your field. Along with time, you will no longer need an extensive marketing campaign and clients will contact you based on your reputation!

In summary, freelancing is more like establishing a business. You spend 70% of the time hunting for projects via internet and the remaining 30% building strong professional relations in the real world.

Advertising

Popular websites can integrate with services such as Google AdSense. Over 90% of Google's $30 billion in revenue each year comes from AdWords, the ads on the right side of the page when you do a search. AdSense allows you to integrate those ads into your website and share the revenue with Google.

MyGameReview.com links to Amazon.com in its video-game write- ups. The company makes a commission every time one of its viewers buys the game on Amazon. AdSense automatically inserts advertisements into a website and pays for every click.

YouTube Partnership

You can also make money by partnering with YouTube. You can post a video and if enough people watch it, YouTube will share some of its advertising revenue with you. Every time someone clicks on one of the ads below or to the right of your video, YouTube will pay you a commission.

Ray William Johnson and Nigahiga have over four million YouTube subscribers and make hundreds of thousands of dollars creating videos for YouTube.

Michelle Phan, for instance, records her makeup tutorials and makes more than many doctors. To upload videos onto YouTube is free, and you can post as many as you want. To join the YouTube Partnership program you have to meet certain criteria (visit YouTube.com for further details).

Private Label Rights

Some companies create information products but allow others to sell them. You can purchase the private-label rights to a website-creation tutorial, for example, for a one-off fee of $200. You can rebrand it as your own, then sell it for $50. You would need four customers to break even.

White Label

White label is used to associate products with a successful brand. The larger company offers the use of its brand, but does not participate in production.

Trading

In the old economy to trade stocks and shares you would usually have to move to a city such as London or New York. Now you can trade stocks, shares or foreign currency through the Internet with companies such as e-trade.com.

Buying stocks is about being able to look at publicly traded companies such as Apple, IBM, Google and Microsoft and predicting if their share price will go up or down. To be successful, you need to study a decent amount of finance, but it is possible to make a decent income trading on the Web. There are many tools available online that enable you to buy and sell virtual shares, allowing you to get some practice without losing any actual money.

Property

You can buy, sell and rent properties through the Internet. Websites in countries such as the U.S. and the U.K. let you know the price of all neighboring houses and what they sold for. For instance, www.foxtons. co.uk gives you a virtual tour of a property so you can see what it looks like.

Websites such as Zillow.com help you find property prices in different parts of the world. The markets in the U.K. and U.S. are usually more defined and transparent, and with higher rates of foreclosures recently there is an opportunity for you to pick up cheap real estate and buy and sell it without visiting the country. This is why establishing trust is so important; people from another part of the world need to know they can rely on your brand, especially when it comes to something as important as a home.

Drop Shipping

Even if you don't have a product yourself, you can do what is known as drop shipping. You receive an order but direct another company elsewhere in the world to buy your product or service. You have no inventory, which means your costs are low. You just pass on the orders when you get them to the appropriate manufacturer. This would be the equivalent of an Amazon.com store receiving an order for a Sony TV, then letting Sony know to send the TV straight from the factory to the customer.

In the pre-Internet economy, you would have had to buy the actual TV, and if you didn't end up selling it, you would lose out. This way you do not have to invest in inventory.

Venture Capital

Through the internet you can become a venture capitalist especially if you live in a wealthier part of the world. Through geo-arbitrage it means your regular income as an accountant might be $3,000 per month. You could take 10% of that income and invest it with an entrepreneur in an emerging part of the world to develop an idea that can go global. This would have been difficult before the internet came along as if you lived in a richer part of the world, you would have needed to finance an entrepreneur from your part of the world and you might not have been able to afford those levels of investment.

You might meet a smart student from a university, for instance, and decide to partner with him or her. You pay the base salary and they do the research and put the business together.

If you get the right people on board, you can eventually build up a good-sized company. Investing in your own business is much more exciting and potentially financially rewarding than putting money into a bank account. Just remember, venture capitalists must be prepared to lose all their money if the idea doesn't work out — and many ideas don't work out. Try to establish your own affordable loss, or an amount you can afford to lose.

You might have a day job that gives you a decent, stable income, but there is an inner entrepreneur inside you. Team up with someone you can afford to hire from a different country and have him or her experiment with your money. While you receive the steady income from your job, your business partner in a different part of the world experiments to help you both make a much bigger income.

9. THE QUICK-START GUIDE TO BECOMING A WEBPRENEUR

If you want to create wealth in the Internet economy, there are three main aspects you must master:

1. **Mindset** – You will face many people who tell you it can't be done. You will have many moments of doubt. You have to stay positive throughout your Webpreneurship journey. If it were easy, everyone would do it. Without the right mindset, even if you do succeed, you will not enjoy it.

2. **Business Knowledge** – Some people think the Internet is some magical machine that spits out money. The business world will always be competitive. You will not make money out of thin air; you still need to provide value. Traditional skills such as marketing, public relations, people management and finance are still important.

3. **Internet Skills** – Your Internet skills are the final component in making a living in the new economy. Define your goals and understand that the Internet is just a tool to help you achieve them. When you to decide to go from Abu Dhabi to Dubai, a car is just the method of transportation. Without a destination, you would just drive around in circles. Use the Internet to build your education or career; that is, get to your destination.
We have developed a wealth-building program at the Webpreneur Academy and are working with educational institutions such as GEMS and Repton to integrate it into their curriculums. Here is an overview:

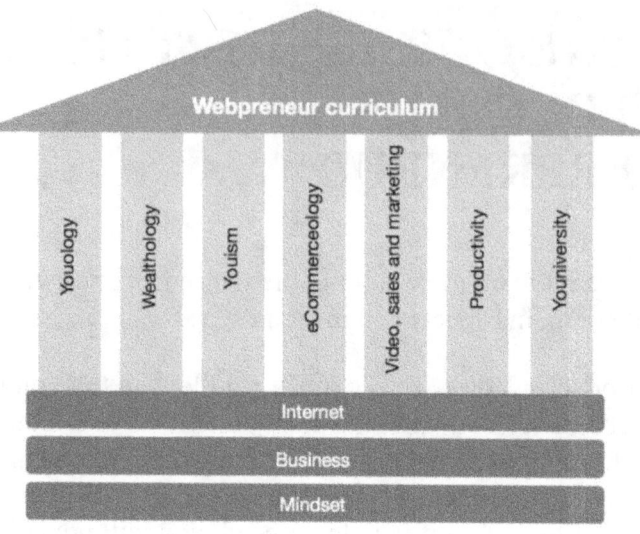

Youology: Know Yourself

"Everybody is a genius. But, if you judge a fish by its ability to climb a tree, it will spend its whole life believing that it is stupid."

                    Albert Einstein

The first step in creating wealth is knowing yourself. If you do not have clear goals, you will not know what direction to go. Draw what is known as a career window. This box helps you to gain perspective on your long- term future.

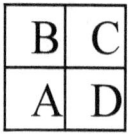

You are in window A today. Ultimately you want to get to D. Often it is not possible for you to jump from A to D in one step. First you might need to go to B, then C before reaching D.

Let's use Amir Anzur's window as an example. While at university, he decided he wanted to be an entrepreneur but didn't think he knew enough about business to start his own. So he crafted a career path from student to entrepreneur:

Accenture	Microsoft, Virgin Media, Oracle, Boots Retail
University	Txfo.com

He joined a management consulting firm (Accenture) straight out of university to gain experience. This allowed him to work with clients such as Microsoft, Virgin Media, Oracle and Boots Retail. He gained the necessary confidence and experience to eventually start his own technology company (Txtfo.com).
A few years after setting up his business in London, Amir decided he didn't feel his work had real meaning. He thought being his own boss would bring him happiness, but it didn't. We stress how important it is to know yourself first, because it will help you get into the right field. A business can take many years to establish, so you might as well be doing something that gives you meaning.

Amir decided meaning would come from helping others create wealth, especially in emerging countries such as Pakistan, where he is from. He had to craft another career window, this one from his own business in London to helping others in emerging countries.

He sold his business, got an MBA and moved to the UAE. He worked at the Knowledge and Human Development Authority, then at the Abu Dhabi Education Council. He learned about education in a country that brought together some of the best teachers in the world, but still got paid. Eventually, he started what came to be known as the Webpreneur Academy.

From entrepreneur to entrepreneur with meaning:

IMD MBA, Switzerland	Knowledge and Human Development Authority, Government of Dubai, Abu Dhabi Education Council, UAE, Ministry of Education, Pakistan
Txtfo, United Kingdom	Webpreneur Academy, United Kingdom and Global

Notice how he didn't make the transition in one step. It took years to go from rain to sunshine, from an entrepreneur to a student to an employee to an educator. He maintained his networks from different parts of the world, rather than starting fresh every time he changed base. Amir physically might have moved from London to Lausanne to Dubai, but his Facebook/ YouTube/LinkedIn friends knew as much about what he was doing as they did about their friends at home. He knew from his career window that he would eventually need these people to help him to reach his goals.

If you are working in sales and marketing for a telecoms company in Kuwait but dream of being a Hollywood actor someday than go chase your dream. Perhaps first get a job in sales and marketing for a telecoms company in Los Angeles. Then get a job in sales and marketing for a movie studio. And from there make your connections to get your big break. Staying where you are and simply dreaming will not make it happen.

The Internet can help you get into almost any industry. You might love football but realize your dream of turning professional is not realistic. But you can start a fan website, interview players on Skype, sell football shirts online or design a football video game. The point is, if you love doing something, it won't feel like work. To win in the Internet economy, you have to put in the time to become the best at what you do; there isn't a lot of easy money.

In the book *Outliers: The Story of Success*, Malcolm Gladwell says it takes 10,000 hours to become an overnight success. Both of us worked many long hours for years before we achieved any real success. Mark Zuckerberg might seem to be an overnight success, but he had a one-on-one programming coach in his teenage years, long before he invented Facebook. Bill Gates started programming when he 13, many years before he founded Microsoft. Focus on your long-term goals because the journey will be a long one.

You might as well enjoy the scenery along the way, so remember to study Youology. The Internet allows you to do what YOU want. To create success in your way. If you don't have passion for what you are doing and just follow the script set by your parents, teachers or boss, your chances of success are lower.

Mark Zuckerberg did not create Facebook so he could make a few million dollars, sell his company and retire on a beach; he has a passion for connecting the world. Steve Jobs did not turn up at work each day so he could increase returns for his shareholders. He was crazy enough to think he could change the world. Bill Gates did not run Microsoft because he wanted the power. At a time when computers were enormous wall-sized contraptions, he had a mission to put a computer in every home; Microsoft has not achieved this but is getting closer. Successful people find their DNA and pursue what is right for them.

Wealthology: Know the Game

You can't win a game unless you understand the rules. The earlier chapters should have familiarized you with how wealth is created. Remember the simple formula for creating wealth:

> Amount of Value You Can Add
> x Number of People You Can Impact
> - Number of People Who Can Do What You Do
> - Cost to Serve
> = Total Wealth Created

All you have to do is simply figure out a way to add value to the world.

The more education and skills you accumulate, the more value you can add. If you know how to touch type, for instance, you can produce content faster.
Figure out ways to impact more people. How can you scale your business? The billionaires of the world have impacted millions. How can you create something that can impact more people?

Adam Smith wrote about specialization. How can you get into a field that few others are in? In the world of medicine, for instance, specialists (such as neurologists) typically earn more than general practitioners. How can you brand yourself so that you are known as the go-to person in your industry?

How can you reduce the cost to serve? Will you pass the savings on to your customers or increase your profit margin and use that money to continue innovating? Perhaps you can hire people in different parts of the world who specialize. The better your personal brand, the more people trust you, enabling you to get down to business faster. You would be more likely to invest in a venture if Bill Gates approached you than a stranger.

Youism: Spread Your Ideas

"Be yourself, everyone else is already taken."
Oscar Wilde, author and playwright

Once you've studied yourself and determined your career goals, you are ready to brand. The Simple Wealth Formula posits that the better your brand is, the fewer people who are perceived to be able to do what you do.

You must be aware of everything that affects your brand. The university you attended, for example, could impact your brand as could your country. Online products that are Made in Nigeria, for example, are harder to sell than Made in California. Don't let this stop you; there are benefits to being where you're from. You can also give the image that you are based in New York, London or Dubai without having to live there.

Imagine we met for a few minutes at an event. If we don't connect through a social network, it will be difficult for us to see what interests we have in common. On Facebook, however, you could see what friends we have in common. On LinkedIn, you could see companies we worked for.

Use online social media tools to build connections, even though it might be years before you do business together. We have people we haven't seen since high school approach us with business opportunities. But since they trusted us then, they are willing to do business with us now.

Wealth in the Internet economy is not simply about money. Your connections are a great asset. Someone with a million followers on Twitter has a resource that could potentially be worth more than a million dollars. If key tastemakers such as Barack Obama, Oprah Winfrey, Nelson Mandela, Mark Zuckerberg, Larry Page (Google) or Sheikh Mohammed (Ruler of Dubai) read your blog, you have the potential to create a great deal of wealth and influence the world.

It used to be difficult to reach CEOs or top politicians. In the Internet economy, you can reach any kingpin of society online with effective marketing. Your opinions matter more than at any other point in history.

You can produce blog posts (articles), YouTube videos or podcasts (audio programs) to build your following. The more fishing poles you have in the water, the more fish you are likely to catch. Similarly, the more content you produce, the more followers you are likely to attract, especially if your content is high-quality. Content is your new fishing pole.

To get started with www.YourName.com as your own domain and website, go to www.HostGator.com. Get a domain and use the open source Content Management Software such as WordPress, Joomla or OpenCart to start your own website.

eCommerce: Do Business Online

"Every one lives by selling something."
                Robert Louis Stevenson, author and poet

In order to make money, you have to actually sell something. You could be an affiliate marketer (e.g., Amazon) who helps others sell things, or you can sell your own products and services.

Students who have studied at the WebpreneurAcademy have ended up selling honey (SabeelHoney.com), skin-care products (MedColl.ie) and freelancing (aamnah.com). These entrepreneurs all had a passion to export something to their part of the world or to import something.

What is your passion? Do you know of any products you want to import or export? You can put up your own website on sites such as ShopMarkaz. com that enable you to get your own domain such as MyOwnShop.com rather than using other people's domain. Remember one of the assets you are building is value of your domain brand over time.

Price the products how you want. You can accept Cash on Delivery (check Aramex.com), PayPal or credit card (check 2Checkout.com or alertpay.com).

Let's imagine you are based in Nigeria and want to target American consumers. Unfortunately, Nigeria doesn't have the best reputation on the Web with Americans. Pakistanis,

Libyans and Yemenis will have similar issues. But you can register a company in the U.S. (for about $600) and make the whole operation seem like it is based in New York. You can visit a website such as Grasshopper.com to get a U.S.-based telephone number that forwards to your mobile or to Skype. You can get a U.S.-based address through companies such as ShopAndShip.com and have your mail forwarded. You will have to file taxes, but the whole set-up costs about $1,000 and should take just a week to set up.

You can also register companies in the UAE through sites such as www.vz.ae. The cost, $10,000 a year, is more expensive than in the U.S., but having a Dubai number and visa might be worth it for people from Afghanistan, Iran, Iraq or Pakistan, which do not have strong global brands. The benefit is also less regulation than the US or Europe and no taxes.

eCommerce will continue to grow as more and more people realize the convenience of shopping via the Web or mobiles. There might be fewer Web-savvy consumers in your part of the world, but there are also fewer competitors. If you focus on being a big fish in a small sea, you will have an advantage when the rest of the world moves into your local market.

Video, Sales and Marketing: Tell the world

"Half the money I spend is wasted; the trouble is I don't know which half."
   –   John Wannamaker, Retailer

Once you have something to sell, you need to tell the world about it. No one will buy from you unless he or she knows about what you have to offer.

In the traditional economy, companies spent millions advertising in newspapers and magazines and on TV and radio and billboards. The problem was no one knew what their return on investment was. Were a million people watching a TV program or were there only 100,000? How many walked out of the room once the commercial began? Was it worth paying $10,000 for a half-page ad on page 3 of Time magazine or on the back cover of Newsweek? It was expensive and hard to target. Amateur advertisers found it hard to get into the game. It wasn't worth the risk for a mom-and-pop shop to make a TV ad because the owners didn't know how many would watch it. It was difficult to start small. But you can start advertising on the Internet with a few dollars, and scale when you know what works. You can measure exactly how many consumers looked at your ad, how many clicked through and in which country they are based.

You can define different ads for different markets and continually test and improve them. Once you spent a few thousand dollars putting up a billboard at the side of a highway, it's difficult to change if it isn't working. You can create high-definition videos to spread your word using a relatively inexpensive video camera or mobile phone. ScreenFlow and Camtasia Studio offer screen-capture software you can use to record a PowerPoint presentation. You can use voice-over if you are uncomfortable in front of the camera, or hire professional voice talent from sites such as odesk.com or voices.com if you don't like the sound of your voice. Now you have a digital product to sell. You can promote it by doing guest posts on other people's blogs or having famous (i.e., well-followed) online personalities interview you. You can use your social media profiles on Facebook and Twitter to sell; remember, if you promote yourself too much, people get annoyed. Think of subtler ways to add value; write a blog post about how to promote a book to attract more followers. Google makes most of its money in advertising. If you do a search on Google, you will see businesses have paid for their ads to appear on the top and right sides of a page.

The advertisers bid for keywords. For instance, a handbag company might offer $1 to Google Adwords for every time someone clicks through to a website after the search: "buy handbags online." If someone bid $1.10 per click, his or her ad would be seen above yours, making it more likely to be clicked on.

In the traditional economy, there was a local phone book that listed phone numbers for plumbers, electricians and hotels. In the Internet economy, more and more people search online for these products and services. You can target your customers more precisely. Someone who types "buy handbags online" is not looking for a plumber, otherwise they would have typed "local plumbers."

The great advantage of the Internet is that it is so measurable. This is where your high school mathematics comes in. If you sell handbags for $60 and your cost to make them is $20, your profit is $40 per sale. For every 10 visitors who visit your website after searching for "buy handbag online," one ends up buying.

You can afford to spend $40/10 visitors = $4 per visitor to visit your site. If you spent $3 per click, you would spend $30 on Google advertising to attract 10 visitors with one of them buying; you would make $40 - $30 = $10 profit. If you spent twice as much you would likely make twice as much profit.

If only one in 100 end up as buyers you can spend $40/100 visitors = $0.40 per visitor. You should bid less than 40 cents for each visit. There is a lot of math involved, but it's not too complicated.

There are two tricks to selling online. First, you need to improve the conversion rate of your website. You want more than one buyer for every 10 visits.

Of course, you also want more people to visit; that is, to increase your traffic. Instead of 100 people visiting per day, how can you make it 1,000? The other way to reach the top of a search on Google is what is known as doing Search Engine Optimization. These are natural search results you do not need to pay Google for. There is an art to this, but basically Google wants to give its users the best experience possible. The company tends to give weight to the number of links to a website.

Wikipedia, for example, is at the top of many search results because many other websites point toward the online encyclopedia as the authority on a subject. The more websites that link to your site, the more authority Google thinks you have. If important websites such as CNN.com or BBC.co.uk link to you, you have even more importance.

Facebook also gets a lot of traffic, and uses the pay-per-click method,

too. Unlike Google, however, Facebook does not use keyword searches to determine its advertising. Instead, it sells advertising based on a user's "likes." On Google, someone might use the search "buy Arsenal shirts," for instance, whereas on Facebook he or she might have joined the group "Arsenal Football Club."

Facebook also allows you to target according to age, gender, country, education and even workplace. A job posting might read: "Women, aged 25 to 35, living in

Jordan, with a university degree who work at HSBC bank."
The more tuned in to your target customer, the more
effective your ad and website can be.

Compare the effectiveness of Google and Facebook to
traditional TV, radio and newspapers. If you were to
advertise pet food, for instance, on a major TV channel you
would pay tens of thousands of dollars for a 30-second
segment. Your ad on pet food would be broadcast to
millions of viewers, many of whom would not even own a
pet. A small percentage of viewers would buy your pet
food, (if they remembered it the next time they went
shopping).

But when you advertise on Google or Facebook, you
already know something about the consumer, either from a
Google search or a Facebook profile. You pay only for
people who are interested enough in your product or
service to click through and visit your website. More and
more people use credit cards to buy online, so the
transaction is often immediate; that is, the consumer won't
forget.
You can target a niche anywhere in the world online.
Maybe you know that women in Saudi Arabia like a special
type of Brazilian skin oil. An online Mexican beauty
website can target Saudi women and sell them a Brazilian
product.

That said, you are still more likely to do business with your
neighbors down the street than someone a few thousand
miles away.

Productivity: Be Effective

If you were asked to dig a hole, would you use a shovel or
a teaspoon? If you are paid a high hourly wage, there is no

incentive to work faster, so you would use the teaspoon. The longer you take, the more money you make.

Bureaucrats often use teaspoons. They get the same salary at the end of the month and if they do their paperwork more effectively, their reward is more paperwork. Effective bureaucrats are either motivated internally or by public recognition.

Entrepreneurs are rewarded for output. They are usually paid by the hole rather than for how long they dig. They would use a shovel, or a digging machine, if they can find one. Entrepreneurs try to do as much as they can in as little time as possible.

Many people do not take the time to improve themselves. They keep doing things the slow way. You should try to be faster online. Learn to touch type, for instance, as it is more efficient than the "hunt and peck" method. If you double your words per minute, you cut your typing time in half.

Remember, your time is valuable, so you want to save it as much as possible. PCs crash more, have lower battery lives and are much slower to use than Macs. Faster Internet connections would also significantly increase your online productivity. If you are always forgetting your passwords, try LastPass.com, a free tool to help you keep track. Want to share big files across many computers? Try dropbox.com. Use sites such as Odesk.com when you don't understand how to do something online. You can fiddle around for hours trying to put your website up, or you can save time and hassle by hiring someone for $7 an hour to do it for you.

Be ruthless with your online time. Do not get stuck in endless chats or Skype conversations. Just because you are not paying a telecommunications company for the call does not mean it is free: time is money. Nothing breaks the workflow like a phone call, an instant message or email. Shut these things off when you are working and you will improve your productivity drastically.

So, you want to become a millionaire? There are eight hours in a regular working day, 40 per week. If you work 48 out of 52 weeks a year, your total working hours would total 1,920.

$1,000,000 / 1,920 = $520 per hour.

You need to generate $520 per hour to make a million dollars in a year. Education (reading this book), and networking can help, but watching cute kittens on YouTube or chatting about the latest celebrity gossip will not.

This is an age of multitasking, but focusing on a single job at a time is much more effective. Try this exercise. Have two of your friends take a piece of paper and draw out three columns. In the first column write down odd numbers (1, 3, 5, 7, 9); in the second, write out the months (January, February, March, April...); in the third, write down even numbers (2, 4, 6, 8, 10).

So the finished page would look like this:

1	January	2
3	February	4
5	March	6
7	April	8
9	May	10
11	June	12

Have one friend work across the columns ("1 January 2," "3 February 4," "5 March 6, etc."). Have the other write down the columns ("1, 3, 5, 7, etc.,") then "January, February, March, etc.," then "2, 4, 6, 8, etc.".

You will notice people doing the single-focused task (i.e., the second way) are able to complete their tasks quicker than those whose brain has to think of an odd number, a month, then an even number. When your brain can focus on one thing at a time, you are a lot more efficient.

In a world that is more and more filled with interruptions and has more and more choices, it is important to be able to focus on your own goals. Do one task at a time. As an entrepreneur you will sometimes feel overwhelmed with all that you can do and should be doing. Focus on the task at hand and do it well.

People often ask if they can start a business when they are still at university or working. You can, but you will have to sacrifice the time you spend watching TV or gossiping with your friends. You will have to be efficient with your time after class or work so you can work on your business. You might even have to sleep a little less.
Watching football or discussing politics with people who have no intention of being in the game won't add much value to the world. Starting a website can have an impact. If you've studied Youology and understand your own goals and dreams, you will want to be more productive. You won't want to waste hours watching endless videos on YouTube.

Productivity is an endless cycle. You have to continually look at your methods and how you can improve them.

YOUniversity: Learn to Learn

More and more ideas are entering society through communication. Printing a book was a big deal a hundred years ago and relatively expensive after the invention of the printing press, but the Internet has made it free to produce and share knowledge.

The way to win in the knowledge economy is to become the best in your niche or industry. In order to become the best, you have to keep track of the latest trends. You must be efficient in the way you consume knowledge.
Let's say you spend half an hour each day commuting to and from work. Most people listen to the news on the radio or music. The problem with news is you can't really control the stock market crash in New York or the war in Iraq. It's a shame if there is an earthquake in Bolivia, but you can't do anything about it. What you can control is what happens inside your circle of influence.

The one hour a day you spend commuting to and from work adds up to five hours a week or 20 hours a month. This is 240 hours a year. This works out at 240 / 8 = 30 full days (i.e, six full weeks) that you could be learning if you were listening to audiobooks. Instead of having to read, listening to an educational book on the way to and from work over a year is the equivalent of six weeks of learning in a university every year. How much more knowledge will that mean for you, especially over your lifetime as you have simply made effective learning time from what you were using to listen to the news or music? Wouldn't that give you a better chance of success in the knowledge economy?

Turning your car into a university is a great way to enhance your knowledge and we strongly encourage you to fill up your mobile phone or car CD player with audiobooks so that you can educate yourself while commuting.

And you no longer have to pay for a lot of university education. You can visit iTunes University and get over

350,000 free lectures from professors at Harvard, Oxford, Stanford and the London School of Economics.
A few hundred years ago, if you did not go to the right university you would not get the right job. Universities had libraries with hundreds of thousands of books. Now anybody can access those books.

Teachers now market themselves by giving away their knowledge via blogs. For instance, visit www.amiranzur.com and you can access plenty of free information. We give out valuable content to show our worth, then make money from seminars and speaking engagements.

You don't have to monetize knowledge, either. Many share what they know for free, to better the world. You can no longer blame your lack of knowledge on your economic station. All of us — governments, corporations and citizens — should help others gain access to the Internet and teach our children to learn to learn.
You have an important tool after you understand the Internet's wealth- creating possibilities. Plumbers can take online courses to become better plumbers. They can also learn to do their own books with online accounting tutorials.

You are not limited to local knowledge. A plumber from Bolivia can learn about best German plumbing practices. You could become the magic plumber of your village by importing these techniques. You can then raise your fees since you are not in direct competition with less-knowledgeable plumbers anymore. They might copy your secrets, but you will be constantly coming up with new ones since you are plugged in to the online international plumbing community.

This is how you truly create wealth. Be the best at what you do. Bring value to the world. The key to being the best is knowledge. Why learn by trial and error on your own, when you could save yourself years of work by learning from someone else?

There was a study to measure what species were able to travel one mile using the least energy. The condor, a type of bird, was at the top and humans were a third of the way down the list. Not at all the most efficient of the Earth's creatures. But then someone compared the condor to the human on a bicycle and humans were far the most efficient of all the species. We have the knowledge and tools to win almost any game!
As humans we continue to improve the way we do things. The Internet can connect you to anyone across the world to gain knowledge, and that is its true power.

10. OUTSOURCING: WEBPRENEUR'S SUCCESS SECRET!

Many of us are familiar with the term "outsourcing" and its uses in today's corporate world. However, when it comes to online business, the practice of this technique is quite different. The best thing is that outsourcing allows you to do a highly successful online business even when you have no relevant experience or in-depth understanding of the products and services you are planning to offer! That is why becoming a renowned entrepreneur (or "webpreneur") does not demand high qualifications and experience.

How Outsourcing Works in Online Businesses?
If you are reading this book, you are definitely one of the motivated people who are determined to figure out the best possible way of creating wealth. To become successful, it is important that you build a strong professional network and benefit the world around you. That is where outsourcing helps. So far, we mainly focused on how you can work individually by using different platforms and marketing yourself. Now, we will concentrate on creating jobs, doing teamwork and making tremendous accomplishments in a limited time.

For instance, you have decided to work as an article writer. You create a good profile on a bidding site and connect with potential clients by sending proposals for some projects. Fortunately, a reputable client hires you for a massive project that demands you to write more than 10 articles of 500 words each in just one week! Keeping aside all your expertise, motivation, and productivity, it is definitely not easy to meet such deadline. Therefore, the best action you can take is to hire some experienced and skilled article writers and assign the project to them. Now,

your workload is shared, and you can quickly meet your client's expectation. In long-term, this will help you build an excellent reputation, take well-paid projects and even charge your clients higher by completing urgent projects successfully. While you are prospering as a businessperson, you are also creating some jobs, improving cash flow and contributing to the betterment of the world economy!
The example discussed above gives a bigger picture of outsourcing. However, if you are not careful enough to make smart decisions at the right time, the outcome may turn out to be a disaster. Let's look at some of the possible problems that may arise and their solutions.

1. Your net income after outsourcing the project is too little.

   It is obvious that when you are hiring someone to do your job, you will need to pay. However, you must keep a track of all the expected costs and transactions just like retail price, sale, and discounts in a physical store. Before even sharing your project with anyone, work out the maximum amount you can reserve for outsourcing after keeping your profit. You must ensure that you are offering a fair price that can attract a skilled and capable person. When mentioning your budget, keep a margin for any negotiations that may take place. Finally, prepare a formal contract that specifies all your conditions, payment terms and project related information for the third-party who is taking your project. These precautions will minimize the chances of any future disputes, financial loss or frauds.

2. Your outsourced employee did not submit the work on time so you missed the deadline.

Emergencies and accidents are natural causes of disturbance and can occur anytime. Therefore, you must keep a room for such events. It is possible that you may not get the work on time, and you end up in a terrible situation where you have nothing to show to your client even after the deadline. To avoid this issue, give your outsourced employee an early deadline for the project. This will allow you to review the work carefully before submitting and even do it from the scratch if necessary.

Also, make sure that you keep an open communication channel throughout. Keep a track of the work and make adjustments in your plan when you foresee some delay.

3. The work quality you got after outsourcing was not up to the required standards.

Several reasons may cause this issue. You may not have provided complete details or explained the project sufficiently. The deadline you gave was too difficult to meet or the person to whom you trusted your project was not capable of handling it. Regardless of the cause, below are some practical measures you should take:

a. Make sure that you conveyed all the necessary information, and there is no room for doubts and misunderstandings. As we are dealing with online communications, it is best to arrange a video call or a meeting if possible. Project discussions should be real-time and active.

b. Instead of demanding to submit the whole project by a particular time, ask to present the work on "installment-basis" i.e. step by step. This will make it easy for you to review. If you find some serious mistakes, you can easily get them corrected and ensure that they are not repeated further.

c. Give upfront payments. If you pay some amount in advance, it will motivate your outsourced employee to work better and fulfill your requirements efficiently.

It is amazing how much money some companies have made by just operating by outsourcing. Some of them include Uber, AppSumo, Careem and Alibaba. After all, this phenomenon encourages you to work in the team or manage a group of people to get your project completed and gain extra profits.

Many times it's difficult to understand something unless you practically experience it. The best way to experience outsourcing in online business is to start with the people you already know and work on some small projects which you can handle alone if any problem arises. Such experience will give you the confidence to implement this idea at a large scale and unfamiliar situations. Once you master this art, you will have no difficulty in completing projects even that are beyond your expertise. This is where you differentiate yourself from your competitors from all around the world!

11. YELLOW SHIRTS VS. RED SHIRTS

Try this simple experiment. Take a group of people from your school or organization and randomly divide them into two groups. Give one group yellow shirts to wear for a few weeks and the other red shirts.

Now watch how communities begin to form. The yellow shirts might start saying things such as: "The red shirts are so arrogant. They never start conversations with us."
Then the red shirts will chime in: "The yellow shirts are not as smart as us. We do all the work. They just copy us."

Even though the teams were chosen randomly, opinions are formed based solely on the color of people's shirts.
This is what the world has become.

We have been randomly divided into countries and religions, professions and skin color. These brands give us a sense of identity.

In the U.K., grown men get into fights over football teams. Is it really worth it to punch someone because he supports Arsenal and you are a Chelsea fan?
In other parts of the world, the fights are over religion or borders that were drawn up long before any of us were born.

Do not judge 300 million Americans because of their president. A leader of the country, whether it's George W. Bush or Barack Obama, does not represent the entire population. In democratic countries, at least 30% of voters support the losing candidate; that is, three out of 10 people do not agree with their country's strategic direction. Presidents and prime ministers get more media coverage, but this will change in the Internet age. Now, any one of the "red" or "yellow" shirts can represent their brands.

A country also should not be judged because a few terrorists did something horrible. Or a race judged because a few commit crime. Or women judged on the clothes they wear, whether it's a burqa or a mini- skirt.
People have the right to live their life with their own culture. The Internet enables us to connect with many types of "weird" people, but don't impose your view of the world on them; appreciate them for who they are. If you want to influence the world, be a good person yourself; others will choose to follow you if you set a good example. Do not go to other parts of the world and try to force people into seeing that your view of the world is right. Once you begin to appreciate different viewpoints, you can begin to appreciate commonalities, too.

Brandism exists and many people will judge you on your religion, nationality or weight; that is, qualities you cannot control. If you want to create true wealth, do not judge people on their brand. If you are Pakistani and do not like working with Indians, you are throwing away a billion potential customers, all because of a line on a map drawn up by bureaucrats decades ago. You might think it doesn't matter what you think about your customers; it is just business, after all, right? The truth is that it shows. It comes out in your work or art.
If you love what you are doing and whom you are doing it with, you will pay attention to the details that matter. If you lack the desire to deal with your clients, the care will not be there and the quality of your product or service will suffer.

In the Internet economy, those who find ways to work with people from different cultures are more likely to be successful. Remember, wealth is created when people exchange different skills. Go to places where you are unique rather than surrounded by your own clones!

End Passportism

The world is now made up of close to 200 countries. A century ago, it was completely different. In 50 years, who knows what the borders will be?
European borders have disappeared over the past few decades, while in Sudan new dividing lines have been drawn. The world keeps shifting, as humans keep erecting artificial barriers and differentiating their brands (i.e., countries)
.

The Internet allows us to live in a world in which we are not judged by the color of our shirt, where a Filipino can make more than an American and a Kenyan bank is more trusted than a Swiss one, where people, products and services will be judged by their quality rather than their stereotype.

In the 1950s, branding was done by skin color in the U.S. Black people were not able to get the jobs white people could. They could not travel. Martin Luther King Jr. had a dream that one day his black children would be able to play with white children and that people would be judged by the content of their character rather than the color of their skin.

The idea of a black president or an African-American TV mogul seemed impossible back then, but in 2008, Barack Obama was elected and Oprah Winfrey hosted the most-popular TV show. Blacks now hold prominent positions in every field, from politics and entertainment to science and literature.

It might be hard to imagine a person from a lower socioeconomic class in your country holding a prominent position, but it will happen. A Brazilian living in Australia might have as much of a chance to lead Germany as a Berliner.

A world without brandism might not be too far away. The Facebook and YouTube generation don't fear unknown brands like our parents did, even if some people still promote distrust. A good place to begin this breaking down of barriers is through sports. It's important to appreciate these contests for what they are: branding exercises. Support your country if you like, but note, too, how each country has its own logo (flags) and theme tune (national anthem).

Remember to always be a positive ambassador for your brand, whether it's your school, workplace, city, country, religion, skin color, gender or even disability. Ultimately you will make it easier or more difficult for the next person from your team to find work. Make sure that whatever shirt you end up wearing benefits.

12. FINAL WORDS FOR THE JEAN- PIERRES AND IMRANS OF THE WORLD

Wealth is created when ideas, products and services are exchanged. Automobiles, trains, phones, newspapers, radio and TV brought great wealth for people in the last century as they allowed us to connect and trade with each other. This century will bring even more wealth as the barriers to entry on the Internet are much lower, meaning even more people will have access to create wealth.

The Internet is a tool that gives us the ability to access billions of people regardless of their geography.
The biggest barrier to entry to the Internet is education. Unless someone shows you exactly what is possible, you won't know what you don't know. Many will miss out on the greatest wealth generation tool in the past 1,000 years. We need to let others see the possibilities of the Internet and how it can be used to greatly improve society's wellbeing.

Remember the Simple Wealth Formula:

> Amount of Value You Can Add
> **x** Number of People You Can Impact
> - Number of People Who Can Do What You Do
> - Cost to Serve
> = Total Wealth Created

Figure out yourself how the Internet can help you with each of the factors. Even if you do not use the Internet, you can still manipulate the factors to generate more wealth.

The Internet brings down barriers so the Imrans of the world have the chance to compete with the Jean-Pierres. Passports and other barriers governments put into place do not prevent people from competing anywhere in the world.

The U.S. was a country that created a tremendous amount of wealth in the past century, mainly because of its investment in infrastructure such as roads, railways and TV. Companies such as Nike faced criticism when they opened shoe factories in countries such as Vietnam when workers in the U.S. were unemployed. But remember, too, the other workers in the U.S. were taking care of a different part of the value chain, creating advertising for local markets and being the face of Nike (e.g., Tiger Woods, Michael Jordan).
Jobs did not disappear, but were spread throughout the world. The Internet is causing the same thing to happen. Your French teacher might actually be based in France; your website might have content written in England, hosted in Germany, and designed in Kenya with products sourced from Japan.

Many Americans complained about how China was taking away its jobs. Companies such as Apple now count China as their second-biggest market and see huge growth there. If you are competitive and ready to fight, then the new economy will create a tremendous amount of wealth for you. If you do not like competing and want to keep the wealth your family obtained through government connections, then the Internet will not so great for you. It will foster transparency, making it easier to detect corruption.

You need to figure out how to deliver value to as many people as possible. You have no excuse of being in the wrong country or not having the right education.

The Internet will help developing countries emerge, and lift millions of people out of poverty faster than at any time in history. To create wealth we need knowledge, and to spread knowledge, there has never been a greater tool than the Internet. A hundred years ago, one teacher could impact a few hundred students. You would have to move to a university in a different part of the world to learn about the latest thinking. Now professors are able to visit your home virtually and teach you at your convenience in any part of the world, many of them for free.

It has never been a better time for the poor to get richer. In the farming economy, you needed to own land in order to be truly wealthy. The most likely way that you could grow your wealth was through inheriting land from your parents, which allowed you to buy even more land and grow your wealth further. If you never inherited land, than it was hard to climb up society. In the industrial economy, the way to get richer was to own a factory. To own land or a factory, you needed a lot of capital in the first place. So chances were if you were born into a poor family, you couldn't afford to get on the ladder to create more wealth.

In the Internet economy, the assets have become ideas and the ability to execute on those ideas. You do not need to buy land or have the capital to set up a factory. A great idea and perseverance will help you create wealth and get to the top of the wealth creation in your society. You do not even need to have money to go to the best schools because if you invest in yourself, you can help yourself get the best education and network to be able to win in this economy. You need to invest in your knowledge, skills, tools, brand and network so that your ability to execute great ideas becomes better and better.

In the Internet economy, we can do more with less. Through our websites www.johnsmith.com and www.amiranzur.com we can reach millions of people; only two decades ago that kind of reach would have required hundreds of employees and business relationships. You, too, can start your own website and start teaching the world.

The Internet also connects you to people across the world who can help you bring change to your local village, whether by buying or selling products and services or exchanging ideas.

Do not look at the Internet economy as a short-term investment, which, if it doesn't work out in a few weeks, it wasn't meant to be. Look at it for the next decade of your life and beyond. Is the Internet going to be an even bigger part of people's lives? Decide for yourself, and, if you are convinced, spend as much time as you can (an hour a day? an hour a week?) discovering how the Internet will work for you. It will take hard work, patience and some trial and error to determine business models and sustainable methods.

As Oscar Wilde said: "Be yourself; everyone else is already taken." What worked for us might not work for you, and what works for you might not work for anyone else. We each have our own DNA, and you have to find yours.

Wealth in the Internet economy is not just about the number you have in your bank account or the car you have in the driveway or the number of rooms you have in your home. These material things are less important as measures of wealth.

Instead: How many views do you have on your YouTube channel? How many followers do you have on Twitter? What unique skills do you have? What languages can you speak? Who is reading your blog? Who can you influence? Who trusts you enough to collaborate or recommend you? These are the new currencies of wealth.

Ultimately, you might not want any of the above. You might be content where you are. That is the ultimate goal, not to win the game by earning the most money but finding fulfillment. Only you can discover how. Remember, the Internet also enables us to lead the lifestyle we desire. You might choose a business model, in the short term, that fits the way you want to live. Longer term, you will be successful once you love what you do.

Our hope is that this book inspires you to take your journey on the Internet to the next level. We hope you now have the confidence that there is a future online for you. You do not need a computer science degree, just a passion to do what you do best and the desire to be the best in the world at it. Use this amazing tool to help your ideas go global or simply dominate the local market.
Unless you jump into the water, it is difficult to learn to swim. Reading is great, but jumping in the pool is what will turn you into a swimmer. Unless you do something with the knowledge you just read, do not expect to have wealth come to you automatically. You must take action and provide value to the world in order for you to get richer.

The Internet has leveled the playing field. The question is: Will you take part in the game or simply watch from the sidelines?

FURTHER READING

To win in the Internet economy, you need to invest in your knowledge. Below are a few great authors and websites to get you going to the next level.

Websites
KhanAcademy.org – An online school
Gutenberg.org – Over 36,000 copyright free books
ecorner.stanford.edu – Lectures by entrepreneurs
Mixergy.com – Interviews with Internet entrepreneurs
Librivox.org – Copyright free audiobooks HostGator.com – Buy your domain, hosting WordPress.com – Set up a free website

Books
Mindset
Unleash the Giant Within, Tony Robbins *The Power of Story*, Jim Lowe
The Alchemist, Paoulo Coehlo
Think & Grow Rich, Napoleon Hill
7 Habits of Highly Effective People, Stephen Covey
Business
Influence Science and Practice, Robert Cialdini
Purple Cow, Seth Godin
Freakonomics, Steven D. Levitt & Stephen J. Dubner
Writing Copy, Robert Bly

Internet
4 Hour Work Week, Tim Ferriss
The World is Flat, Thomas Friedman *The Long Tail*, Chris Anderson *Don't Make Me Think*, Steve Krug

END NOTES

1. 2010 Per Capita GDP from "World Bank, World Development Indicators"
2. www.data360.org/dsg.aspx?Data_Set_Group_Id=80
3. Jan. 30, 2012. General Motors (employees: 209,000, Valuation: $38 billion). McDonald's (employees: 400,000. Valuation: $100 billion). Facebook (employees: 3,000. Valuation: $75 billion – 100 billion). Sources: Finance.yahoo.com and Wikipedia.
4. http://articles.cnn.com/2008-03-06/politics/democrats.campaign_1_ clinton-campaign-campaign-funds-michigan-and-florida-delegations?_s=PM:POLITICS
http://voices.washingtonpost.com/44/2008/11/obama-raised-half-a- billion-on.html
http://articles.latimes.com/2008/mar/07/nation/na-money7
5. http://www.internetworldstats.com/stats.htm
6.   https://www.startupgrind.com/blog/these-8-successful-companies-were-built-using-outsourced-developers/